Indiana Sporting Life

Selections from *Traces of Indiana and Midwestern History*

INDIANA HISTORICAL SOCIETY PRESS

INDIANAPOLIS 2005

© 2005 Indiana Historical Society Press

Printed in China

This book is a publication of the

Indiana Historical Society Press

450 West Ohio Street

Indianapolis, Indiana 45202-3269 USA

www.indianahistory.org

Telephone orders 1-800-447-1830

Fax orders 1-317-234-0562

Order online @ shop.indianahistory.org

Library of Congress Cataloging-in-Publication Data

Indiana sporting life : selections from Traces of Indiana and Midwestern history / [editor,
    Ray E. Boomhower].
        p. cm.
    ISBN 0-87195-186-X (alk. paper)
    1. Sports–Indiana–History. 2. Athletes–Indiana–Biography. I. Boomhower, Ray E.,
1959- II. Indiana Historical Society.

GV584.I5I53 2005
796'.09772–dc22   2005052002

INDIANA
SPORTING
LIFE

Selections from
*Traces of Indiana and
Midwestern History*

CONTENTS

 # editors' page

In their book *After the Fact,* historians James West Davidson and Mark Hamilton Lytle advise their readers that when historians neglect the literary aspect of their discipline, when they "forget that good history begins with a good story," they risk losing the wider audience that all "great historians have addressed." Since joining the Indiana Historical Society in 1987, it has been my privilege—first as the Society's public relations coordinator, then a contributing editor and writer, and now as managing editor—to be involved with the numerous "good stories" that have appeared in the pages of *Traces* magazine.

These stories have often been told with specific themes in mind. What follows in this book are articles from past issues of *Traces* that follow the theme of "Indiana Sporting Life." Subsequent books will focus on other themes examined in the magazine. The writers who crafted these pieces showcase the distinguished lineage of this award-winning quarterly produced by the Society and distributed as a benefit of membership in the organization.

Created in 1989, *Traces* has been an instrument for the Society to bring to its members good narrative and analytical history about the Hoosier State in its broader contexts of region and nation. Through the years and thanks to the unstinting efforts of its first managing editor, J. Kent Calder, and such valuable staff members as Megan McKee, George Hanlin, Judith McMullen, and Rachel Popma, the magazine has examined the impact of Hoosiers on the nation and the world by exploring the work of such nationally-known figures as Eugene Debs, Gene Stratton-Porter, Lew Wallace, James Dean, Madam C. J. Walker, and Wendell Willkie. The magazine also has studied the influence on the state of non-Hoosiers such as H. L. Mencken, John Muir, and Harry Truman. Just as important to the magazine's staff, *Traces* has also featured ordinary Indiana men and women, shedding light on obscure lives and work.

Traces has continued over the years to attract readers and fulfill its mission to provide nonfiction articles that are solidly researched, engagingly written, and amenable to illustration. One way it does so is by attracting to its pages an eclectic group of writers, including such nationally known authors as Stephen Ambrose, William Styron, and Nicholas von Hoffman. The magazine has also called upon the talents of a wide variety of local writers, including academics, journalists, and public historians. One of *Traces*'s strengths is its ability to nurture new talent and develop long-term relationships with its contributors.

In working with our variety of contributors I try to keep in mind advice given by the writer John Jerome, who once noted that from an author's point of view an editor's first job is to assist in the execution of the writer's intent. "If the writer's intent is wrong," said Jerome, "then a good editor tries to refocus that intent, to cajole or tease or somehow seduce the writer into a better one." I look forward to cajoling and teasing writers for many years to come in order to produce a magazine that appeals to anyone interested in the nineteenth state's past.

Ray E. Boomhower

Everett Case

Conquers Dixie: Hoosier Basketball in North Carolina
Jim L. Sumner

9

For many people around the country, the word *Hoosier* is synonymous with basketball. Indiana high school and college basketball have long been known for excitement and excellence. The image of the Indiana farm kid practicing jump shots into the night has been indelibly impressed on the country's collective sports consciousness by television, movies, and books.

Some of Indiana's greatest basketball talents have spread the state's passion for hoops to other parts of the country. One of the best known is Martinsville's John Wooden, a great player at Purdue in the 1930s who founded the University of California, Los Angeles (UCLA), dynasty that dominated college basketball in the 1960s and 1970s. Even before Wooden went west, however, another Indiana transplant was plowing distant fields. Shortly after the conclusion of World War II, basketball evangelist Everett Case went into North Carolina and helped create a tradition that has made Tobacco Road as much a mark of basketball excellence as Hoosier and has inspired North Carolina universities in capturing numerous National Collegiate Athletic Association (NCAA) men's basketball titles.

Everett Norris Case was born in Anderson, Indiana, on June 21, 1900. He grew up in that city, only six blocks from the high school. Case played tennis and was an active member of the Student Athletic Council. He coached a Methodist church youth basketball team. The one thing he couldn't do was play basketball, at least on the scholastic level. The diminutive Case wasn't big enough or good enough to play for the high school team. Ironically, one of the best basketball coaches of all time never played a game of organized basketball. Yet growing up in Anderson—called "the hottest basketball town on earth, the epicenter of grass-roots basketball" by writer Phillip Hoose—Case could hardly have failed to absorb a passion for basketball.

After graduating from Anderson High School Case took a position as assistant basketball coach at Connersville High School. Like many teachers during this period, he worked on a college degree during the summers at a number of schools in the Midwest. Eventually he would acquire not only a bachelor of arts from Central Normal College in Danville, Indiana, but also a master of arts from the University of Southern California. His thesis was titled "An Analysis of the Effects of Various Factors on Accuracy of Shooting Free Throws." Case concluded that the underhand method was superior.

By the time Case earned his master's degree in 1934 he had established himself as an authority in more areas of basketball than just foul shooting. The young Case was something of a nomad the first few years after high school. He left Connersville following the 1920 season to become head coach at Columbus High School. Barely out of his teens, Case coached that team to a 20–10 record. Clearly he had some aptitude for coaching. The following season he was at Smithville High School. He coached that club to a superb 32–6 mark.

In February of 1922, as Case was wrapping up his only season at Smithville, Frankfort High School was gutted by a fire. A new gym, Howard Hall, was dedicated in November of that year. Along with the new gym, Frankfort would have a new coach. Everett Case would elevate the Frankfort High School Hot Dogs to the highest level of Indiana high school basketball. Case won 24 games his first year in Frankfort. His second team went 26–2 and advanced to the state finals, where they lost to Martinsville 36–30. In 1924–25, Case's third year, the Hot Dogs went 27–2 and beat Kokomo 34–20 in the state finals, the first of Case's four Indiana state championships.

Case continued winning games and titles at Frankfort. In the process he became known as a fiercely competitive, innovative coach, who was always prepared and would do almost anything to win. He asked his players to sign a pledge to eat the right foods, get to bed early, and even wear hats against the Indiana winter, the better to protect against colds.

LEFT: While in high school, Case coached a Methodist church youth team. **RIGHT:** Coach Case's Frankfort Hot Dogs won the 1936 state championship. Front row: Loren Joseph, Ralph Vaughn, Coach Everett Case, Jay McCreary, and James Miner; back row: Merlin Goodnight, Glenwood Witsman, Ralph Montgomery, John Slaven, Max Livezey, and Ansel Street.

Case's clubs were well-conditioned teams that could run all night. He preferred up-tempo, fast-break basketball. However, he would drop that tactic, or any other, in order to enhance his chances of winning. In January 1927 a visiting Logansport team was stranded by a snowstorm. By the time it arrived in Frankfort, it was almost midnight. The game started anyway. At that time basketball had no ten-second line. Case's club used the entire floor to hold the ball in an attempt to force its exhausted guests out of their zone defense. When Logansport stayed in the zone, Frankfort stayed in its delay game. Frankfort escaped with a 10–7 victory. Postgame fistfights erupted throughout the stands. After another slowdown win at Bedford angry fans pelted the floor with food and trash to protest Case's stall.

The hostility directed toward Case wasn't just because of his tactics or his incessant winning. Longtime *Indianapolis Star* columnist Bob Collins wrote in 1982 that Case coached in Indiana during "the wild and wooly days when rules consisted of what you could get away with." If so, Case certainly was at home. It was argued widely that he and a network of Frankfort boosters recruited across the state. These rumors were not just sour grapes. The Indiana High

School Athletic Association suspended Frankfort for the first half of the 1928–29 season for attempting to induce two players to transfer across the state from Jennings County. Frankfort recovered in time to win its second state title, beating Indianapolis Technical 29–23 in the finals. Despite the censure, Case's program continued to be plagued by rumors of illegal recruiting throughout his high school tenure. Some Case supporters argue, however, that players were attracted only by Case's coaching reputation.

In 1931 Case was lured back to his hometown. Success followed him back to Anderson, as did controversy. His Anderson team was placed on probation for the 1932–33 season for using an ineligible player and violating "the spirit and purpose of the rules." The ineligible player, Joe Hallinan, had recently moved from Akron, Ohio, to Anderson. It was rumored that he had played semiprofessional basketball in the Buckeye state.

Perhaps Case decided to lie low for awhile, or perhaps he simply wanted to get away from midwestern winters. Following the 1933 season Case left Anderson to go to the University of Southern California and finish his graduate degree. While there he assisted Sam Barry in coaching the Trojans.

Barry's son Rick would later become a standout basketball player. Significantly, Rick Barry, one of the game's great foul shooters, was the last National Basketball Association (NBA) player to use the underhand method favored by Case.

Case returned to Indiana in the fall of 1934. He came back to Frankfort, however, rather than Anderson. After a mediocre 17–12 record, Case coached Frankfort to his third state title in 1935–36. This team lost early in the season to Tipton and played a tie against Indianapolis Technical, in which both coaches agreed to call the game after two overtimes (the rules later were amended to prohibit ties). Frankfort didn't lose again. In fact the team was rarely challenged. The Hot Dogs mauled Anderson 34–18 and Fort Wayne Central 50–24 in the final two games for the state title. This club, regarded as one of the best in Indiana prep history, was led by Ralph Vaughn, who later starred at the University of Southern California, and Lawrence "Jay" McCreary, who would spark Indiana University to the 1940 NCAA title with 12 points in the finals against the University of Kansas.

In 1938–39 Case became the first man to win four Indiana state titles at the same school when his Frankfort club defeated Franklin 36–22 in the state finals. Case came close to winning a fifth title in 1942, as Frankfort fell to eventual champ Washington in the semifinals.

Case joined the U.S. Navy in 1942 as a lieutenant. He never coached high school ball again. He finished his prep coaching career with a record of 467–124–1, including 385–99–1 at Frankfort. Some sources credit Case with 726 wins, but that total is certainly inflated. Over a twenty-one-year career, this would average over 34 wins per season. However, Case only won more than 30 games once, a 32–6 mark in 1921–22 in Smithville.

The navy knew what to do with Everett Case. He served in a number of stateside postings, most of which took advantage of his skills. He coached the DePauw Naval Training Station team to a 29–3 record

in 1944–45 and coached the Ottumwa (Iowa) Naval Air Station team to a 27–2 mark in 1945–46.

Perhaps the war expanded Case's horizons. In any event he decided not to return to the Hoosier high school wars. He considered staying in the navy but decided to make a bold move south. In the spring of 1946 Case accepted a position as head coach at North Carolina State College (now University), in the state capital of Raleigh. At the time he accepted the position, Case had never set foot in Raleigh.

State officials were put on Case's trail by Chuck Taylor, who, as a spokesman for Converse Shoe Company, traveled across the country, putting on clinics. No one knew the state of basketball better than Taylor, a Columbus, Indiana, native, and Taylor recognized Case as a man of rare ability.

Case certainly faced a challenge. North Carolina State was the land-grant school in North Carolina. The University of North Carolina (UNC), located twenty-five miles northwest of Raleigh in Chapel Hill, looked down on State as a "cow college," an opinion shared by nearby private schools Duke University and Wake Forest College. Certainly, State had done little on the athletic fields to change this opinion. A limited academic curriculum, poor facilities, and relative neglect by the state legislature had led to years of high coaching turnover and athletic mediocrity. Nowhere was this more apparent than in basketball. Historian Bill Beezley has written that State fans "probably got more thrills from crossword puzzles than basketball" prior to Case's arrival. Yet, State officials thought that basketball had potential at the school. Compared to football, basketball required smaller squads and less money. Before the war State had begun construction of Reynolds Coliseum, a new basketball arena which, when completed in 1949, would be the largest in the state. When Case arrived it was just a shell, but the implications were obvious: the school had made a commitment to big-time basketball.

Case had a galvanizing effect on basketball, not just at North Carolina State but throughout North

Hotly recruited by both Coach Adolph Rupp and Coach Case, Ronnie Shavlik chose North Carolina State over Kentucky.

Carolina. Shortly after he came to Raleigh, modifications were made to Reynolds that increased its potential seating capacity to 12,400, making it the largest such facility in the South. Case quickly put together an almost completely new team. Not surprisingly, he relied heavily on players from his native state, many of whom were military veterans. Of the ten freshmen he brought to State, six were from Indiana. The most talented of these imports was Dick Dickey, a forward from Alexandria. Another addition was Norm Sloan, of Lawrence Central High School, near Indianapolis. Harold "Whitey" Snow of Anderson joined the team, though he had played professional basketball for the Anderson Packers the season before. Snow was able to play because he had signed no contract with the professional team. Case introduced a fast-paced, high-scoring game that overwhelmed opponents and enthralled fans. Before long these "Hoosier Hotshots" were the terrors of the Southern Conference.

The 1946–47 season was one of the most tumultuous in North Carolina State history. State had difficulty finding early season opponents, since many of the North Carolina schools rarely played before Christmas. Case put together a schedule that included military teams, amateur clubs, and two Indiana colleges, Anderson College and Franklin College. By the time most Southern Conference teams began their seasons, State had already played eleven games and won nine of them. One of these victories was a 58–42 win over a Holy Cross team that would go on to capture the NCAA championship. When State defeated archrival University of North Carolina 48–46 in overtime in Chapel Hill, State fans were ecstatic.

The only problem was that few people could watch Case's exciting team. While construction continued on the new coliseum, State played its home games in Thompson Gym, capacity approximately 3,400. Before the war this modest facility was rarely filled. However, State, like most other colleges and universities, was inundated by a postwar enrollment explosion. Before the season began both State and UNC announced that student demands would fill most seats. Most State games were standing room only. On February 25 so many people crowded Thompson Gym for the rematch with UNC that fire marshals refused to allow the game to take place. Angry State students vented their frustrations by setting off fire alarms across campus. This kind of passion over a basketball game may have been common in Indiana, but it was unheard of in North Carolina in 1947.

Fearing a repeat, Southern Conference officials hastily moved the postseason tournament from Raleigh's 3,500-seat Memorial Auditorium to the more spacious 9,000-seat Duke Indoor Stadium in Durham. State went on to capture the Southern Conference title, defeating Maryland, George Washington, and UNC, the latter by a 50–48 score. This was State's first Southern Conference title since 1929 but would not be its last. State did not get an invitation to the NCAA tournament (only eight teams did in 1947) but did go to the New York-based National Invitational Tournament (NIT), which then was at least as prestigious as the NCAA tournament. Case's team defeated St. John's, lost to Kentucky, and

LEFT: Gary, Indiana, native Sammy Ranzino shoots against Colgate in the December 1950 Dixie Classic title game, won 85–76 by State. **RIGHT:** NC State's 1949 Southern Conference champions. Vic Bubas of Gary, Indiana, is wearing the net around his neck, and Dick Dickey of Alexandria is seated far right.

defeated West Virginia for third place. His first season in Raleigh was a spectacular 26–5. By comparison the previous four State teams had won a mere 28 games combined, against 45 losses.

Case's inaugural campaign in Raleigh was simply a prelude. His second team was bolstered by the arrival of high-scoring Sammy Ranzino, a native of Gary, Indiana. A six foot, two inch forward, Ranzino would become one of State's greatest players. Ranzino later gave some insight into how Case worked his home state: "I never knew where North Carolina was, really. When Coach Case came to talk to me, I asked where NC State was. He said it was where all the good Indiana players were going." Also arriving that year was another Gary import, Vic Bubas, a man who would figure in the basketball lore of Tobacco Road for decades to come. Led by Dickey and Ranzino, State spent part of the season ranked number one in the wire service polls. Fire marshals canceled another home game, this time against Duke University, after which State moved its home games off campus to Memorial Auditorium. State was defeated only twice in the regular season, a four-point loss to West Virginia and a controversial overtime loss to Holy Cross in the Sugar Bowl Tournament in New Orleans, when officials mistakenly awarded a State basket to Holy Cross.

The Wolfpack captured the Southern Conference title again but was upended in the first round of the NIT by DePaul when mumps kept Dickey out of the game. It ended the season at 29–3.

Dickey and Ranzino led State to a 25–8 record in 1949 and its third consecutive Southern Conference title. The Wolfpack repeated its conference championship in 1950, 1951, and 1952, an astonishing and unprecedented six consecutive championships. Case's 1953 club lost 71–70 in overtime to Wake Forest in the conference tournament finals.

State's program was at its peak during these years. Conference titles, all-Americans, and high national rankings enabled State fans and alumni to strut their proverbial stuff as never before. The one title that eluded Case was the national championship. During much of this period only one team from the southeast region could be invited to the NCAA tournament, and Kentucky's Adolph Rupp, the Baron of the Bluegrass, considered this invitation his for the asking. Kentucky won the NCAA title in both 1948 and 1949, while State sat on the outside looking in. In 1950 Case offered to play Rupp in a sort of quasi-playoff for the right to play in the NCAA. Although there were precedents for such an arrangement, Rupp refused to have anything to do with State. The NCAA committee called Rupp's bluff and selected State. State won its opening match against Bob Cousy's Holy Cross team but lost in the semifinals (not yet called the Final Four) 78–73 to City College of New York. CCNY went on to win the title, while State won the consolation game for third place. This would be the closest Case would come to an NCAA title. Rupp and Case never made amends.

In 1951 the tournament was expanded to sixteen teams. State made it back to the NCAA that season but was handicapped by an arcane NCAA rule that allowed freshmen to play varsity ball but only permitted players to be eligible for the NCAA tournament three seasons. Thus seniors Ranzino, Bubas, and Paul Horvath, all of whom had played as freshmen in 1947–48, were ineligible for the 1951 tournament. Minus its three stars, State pulled a remarkable upset in the first round, beating Villanova 67–62. Case later called it his greatest win. The outmanned Wolfpack lost the next game to Illinois. State's 1952 NCAA journey ended in its first game against St. John's. The Redmen were coached by Frank McGuire, a man who would loom large in Case's future.

Case was busy not just winning basketball games but also promoting the game he loved. He became a regular speaker at civic affairs across the state. His greatest innovation came in 1949 and was directly related to the opening that fall of Reynolds Coliseum. Case was convinced that several of his close losses could be attributed to "homer" officiating. His solution was to bring the top teams to Raleigh, a possibility now that State had a showplace arena. He came up with the Dixie Classic, a three-day, eight-team tournament held during the interval between Christmas and New Year's Day. The format was simple. North Carolina's so-called Big Four—North Carolina State, the University of North Carolina, Duke, and Wake Forest—would host four outside schools. The winners would play each other, and eventually a champion would be crowned. Over the years the Dixie Classic would become a holiday fixture,

attracting attention across the country and luring such prominent basketball schools as Holy Cross, Seton Hall, Oregon State, Iowa, Louisville, Dayton, and Michigan State. In 1958 the University of Cincinnati, led by the great Oscar Robertson from Crispus Attucks High School in Indianapolis, came to Raleigh ranked number one and left with a pair of hard-fought losses. Case's Wolfpack captured the Dixie Classic title seven times in its twelve-year run.

Case's success gave State an unprecedented publicity bonanza. In 1951 the *Saturday Evening Post* wrote a glowing report titled "Basketball Bug Bites Dixie." The same year the *Raleigh News and Observer* named Case "Tar Heel of the Week," an honor usually reserved for politicians or business leaders. The influential paper recognized Case's impact: "Since the little man came here from Indiana . . . basketball has almost supplanted politics as the favorite topic of discussion in the North Carolina capital. This interest . . . is evident all across the State, which has reacted by building scores of additional high school gyms and insisting on better coaching material. Game attendance has picked up everywhere and makeshift goals have been erected in the most unlikely places—on trees, on the sides of barns, in tobacco warehouses—where budding collegiate stars spend their weekends working to perfect their basketball technique."

In 1954 Case had a new playground. Following the conclusion of the 1953 academic year the Big Four, along with the University of Maryland, the University of South Carolina, and Clemson University, left the Southern Conference to establish the Atlantic Coast Conference; the University of Virginia joined the following year. Case gave early evidence that he would dominate the ACC as easily as he had laid waste to the Southern Conference. His 1953–54 team won 28 games and captured a thrilling first ACC tournament title, defeating North Carolina by one point, Duke by four points, and Wake Forest by two points (in overtime) for the title. State lost in the NCAA to eventual national champion La Salle and its all-American Tom Gola.

North Carolina State Archives

Vic Bubas poses in 1949 wearing the Wolfpack's number seventy-four; later in his career he switched to seventy-eight.

However, there were clouds on the horizon for Case and North Carolina State. In a very real sense he was a victim of his successes. His ACC rivals worked assiduously to catch up with the Wolfpack behemoth. Rival North Carolina lost to Case an agonizing fifteen straight times. Fed up with these galling losses to a school it considered its inferior, UNC fought back by hiring Frank McGuire, the same man who had ended Case's 1952 season. The feisty McGuire tapped into his own recruiting pipeline, this one leading south from New York City, and quickly brought that school back into the basketball spotlight. Duke, Wake Forest, and Maryland also elevated their programs, upgrading facilities and spending more money

on recruiting than had previously been the case.

Case's recruiting skills also caused him problems. Emboldened by constant winning and refusing to settle for second best, Case bent the rules, just as he had in Indiana. Recruiting high school basketball players to colleges was just as competitive in the 1950s as it is today, although not as well publicized. Case's favorite tactic was to invite prospects to highly competitive tryouts. Although legal in the 1940s, this procedure was controversial. In 1948 L. V. Phillips, Commissioner of the Indiana High School Athletic Association, declared that these tryouts violated that group's prohibition of off-season basketball. Phillips informed Case that "Indiana is proud of its basketball and is opposed to this state being turned into a 'farm system' for Mr. Case or any other coach."

Case feigned ignorance and replied that he had no intention of circumventing Indiana high school regulations. The incredulous Phillips responded: "When this letter is published in our official bulletin, I am sure the reference to Mr. Case's ignorance of the rules will make both interesting and amusing reading for school officials and fans in the Hoosier state."

In the early 1950s the NCAA outlawed the tryout system. However, it had been good to Case, and he saw no reason to change. In 1954 the NCAA placed the Wolfpack on probation for the 1954–55 season, primarily for conducting tryouts. Some of these tryouts had involved Case's star recruit, Ronnie Shavlik, a six foot, eight inch scoring machine from Denver, Colorado. Case had outrecruited Rupp for Shavlik's services, and Case always suspected Rupp of turning him in. Rupp consistently refused to play State, and by all accounts the two giants developed a genuine animosity toward each other. Although the Wolfpack captured the 1955 ACC title, it was prohibited from going to the NCAA tournament. Runner-up Duke went instead.

Case was nothing if not resilient. Shavlik turned out to be as good as advertised. State captured the 1956 ACC title and finished the regular season ranked second in the country. Unfortunately, Shavlik broke his wrist in the tournament finals against Wake Forest. He valiantly attempted to play with his wrist in a cast in State's NCAA match against Canisius. He scored 25 points but underdog Canisius won 79–78 in four overtimes. Case called it the "toughest game I ever lost."

The loss to Canisius marked the conclusion of Case's first decade at State. All in all it was a remarkable ten years. His teams compiled a 267–60 record and captured the Southern Conference or ACC title nine times, losing the tenth by one point. However, the Canisius loss also signaled a downturn for Case in Raleigh. The next season his Wolfpack limped to a listless 15–11 mark. The plaudits instead went to rival North Carolina. Starting five New Yorkers, Frank McGuire's Tar Heels compiled a perfect 32–0 mark, capturing the NCAA title that forever eluded Case.

UNC's success was the least of Case's worries during the 1956–57 season, however. In the fall of 1956 the NCAA hit State with a massive four-year probation that prohibited all State teams, not just the basketball team, from participating in postseason play. Again Case's recruiting zeal had gotten the best of him. The target this time was Louisiana prep phenom Jackie Moreland. The NCAA determined that State had made a number of illegal offers to Moreland, including a seven-year scholarship (including medical school) for his girlfriend. Case protested his innocence and Moreland, who died of cancer in 1971, offered numerous contradictory testimonies to NCAA officials. Nonetheless, the probation, the most severe in NCAA history at the time, stuck. It kept Case's 1958–59 ACC champions from competing in the NCAA. This club, which featured ball-handling wizard Lou Pucillo, finished the season 22–4. It captured Case's last Dixie Classic title, beating Cincinnati with Oscar Robertson and Michigan State with its all-American Johnny Green. It would be Case's last twenty-win season.

During the 1950s the wily Case was known as the

"Old Gray Fox." During the early 1960s he simply seemed old, as much of the competition had passed him by. In addition to North Carolina's perennial powers, Duke had become a powerhouse. Vic Bubas, who had remained at State as Case's right-hand man following his graduation, moved down the road to Duke in May 1959. The following spring Bubas's Blue Devil team captured the ACC title, the first of many for that school. Farther west in Winston-Salem, Wake Forest was preparing for its best years, under the tutelage of colorful coach Horace "Bones" McKinney. In 1962 Wake Forest would advance to the NCAA Final Four, along the way introducing guard Billy Packer to a national audience. McGuire continued to recruit the cream of New York's prep crop to Chapel Hill. Faced with this kind of competition, an outmanned State team struggled to a shocking 11–15 mark in 1959–60.

The final blow to the Case empire came in the 1960–61 season. During the season several curious State performances raised Case's suspicions. In an early contest against Georgia Tech, the Wolfpack lost most of a 26-point second half lead, before holding on for a 6-point win. Case had seen enough basketball to know when a team wasn't giving its best effort.

In the early 1950s the world of college basketball had been rocked by a nationwide point-shaving scandal in which players accepted money from gamblers to ensure that their teams kept the scoring margin beneath a certain agreed-upon spread. No North Carolina schools were involved in this scandal, and Case aimed to keep it that way. He regularly invited law enforcement representatives to talk to his club about gamblers. These efforts fell short. Four State players, Don Gallagher, Stan Niewierowski, Anton Muehlbauer, and Terry Litchfield, accepted money from gamblers to shave points in several games during the 1960–61 season.

Everett Case normally was the most optimistic of men. Norm Sloan has written that Case "always looked like he had just gotten out of bed and was full of life, always going in high gear." Yet even Case's will couldn't carry him past this hurdle. He never recovered from the point-shaving scandal. University officials eliminated the Dixie Classic and restricted recruiting at both State and UNC, which also had players involved. State won only 29 games in the three seasons following the scandal. In 1962 Case was diagnosed as suffering from myeloma, cancer of the bone marrow. Yet Case continued to coach until the beginning of the 1964–65 season, when he was forced to resign after the second game, a disappointing loss to Wake Forest. The close contest had left

and promoted the game relentlessly. Case did not build just a team; he built a program. He upped the basketball ante and forced his opposition to follow suit. Several of Case's former players became top college coaches. Included in that group are Hoosiers Bubas, who took Duke to three Final Fours in the 1960s, and Sloan, who coached his alma mater to the 1974 NCAA title. Most important, Case made fans of casual observers and made these fans care passionately about the sport. For much of the 1950s State led the NCAA in total attendance. Case's occasional walks

The final blow to the Case empire came in the 1960–61 season. During the season several curious State performances raised Case's suspicions.

Case weak and dizzy. His final record at State was 377–134. Case's health worsened until his death on April 30, 1966. The Old Gray Fox had one last surprise. Although the lifelong bachelor left the bulk of his estate to his sister Blanche, he also left shares to fifty-seven former State basketball players, every living player who had earned a degree. This group included Dickey, Bubas, Sloan, and Ranzino.

Everett Case didn't invent basketball or introduce it to North Carolina. The game was played in that state prior to Case's arrival, and played well, at least on occasion. For example, UNC's undefeated 1924 club was voted national champs by the Helms Athletic Foundation, while the 1946 Tar Heel club finished second in the NCAA tournament to Oklahoma A&M. But the sport attracted little attention and generated little enthusiasm before the arrival of Case. No one in the Tar Heel state had put such a complete package together as did the Old Gray Fox. To borrow a phrase from football, Case was a "triple threat." He coached an exciting brand of basketball, recruited talented players well-suited to play that brand of ball,

on the wrong side of the rule book also set an example that has been followed too often; North Carolina State has been under NCAA probation under Case's successors Sloan and Jim Valvano.

Everett Case has been honored numerous times. He is a member of the Naismith Memorial Basketball Hall of Fame, the North Carolina Sports Hall of Fame, and the Indiana Basketball Hall of Fame. Frankfort High School now plays in Case Arena, while North Carolina State has its Case Athletic Center. The most valuable player in the Atlantic Coast Conference Tournament is awarded the Everett Case Award.

In a perhaps apocryphal story Everett Case was once congratulated on a successful season. He is said to have told his admirer that he would only be a success when he saw a basketball hoop nailed to every barn and tree in North Carolina. Before he died he came close to seeing that dream fulfilled. In less than two decades in North Carolina, Everett Case successfully transplanted Hoosier Hysteria to his adopted state and helped make basketball a way of life in North Carolina.

The King of Speed

Erwin G. "Cannon Ball" Baker

Ray Featherstone

On March 12, 1882, Erwin G. Baker was born in a four-room log house near the town of Weisburg in southeastern Indiana. Give his humble beginnings and sixth-grade education, few would have guessed that he would make much of a name for himself. Years later, however, he had achieved world-wide fame, so much so that upon meeting him, President Herbert Hoover declared, "Mr. Cannonball, I believe that more people know your name than they do that of the President of the United States."

Baker, who stood six feet, two inches tall and weighed more than 200 pounds in his prime, achieved his fame by competing in the in the rough-and-tumble world of motorcycle, automobile, and endurance racing. Hoosier journalist Ernie Pyle noted that Baker achieved his records with little sleep, existing on a diet of "steak, hash-browned potatoes, and black coffee." The only person to race at the Indianapolis

money, he bought an old one-cylinder Indian motorcycle to "just to get around" with.

A few years after moving to Indianapolis, Baker, known as "Bake" to his friends, joined the Southside Turners, where he met the fitness club's champion acrobat, Bill Irrang. The two paired up for a few years, performing on vaudeville stages throughout the country. For one of the duo's tricks, Baker kept eleven punching bags going at one time while Irrang somersaulted over ten chairs. By 1906, though, Baker had tired of the vaudeville circuit and returned to Indianapolis. He again worked as a machinist, saved his money, and purchased a new motorcycle. Joining a local motorcycle club, he became a familiar figure on the group's numerous outings.

Baker's first recorded venture into competitive racing came in 1908 on an Indian motorcycle at Crawfordsville. It was the Fourth of July and the Elks

Baker's record prompted a telegram from Henry Ford himself, who said, "Congratulations, wonderful run." In recalling the telegram with a reporter, Baker laughingly said that Ford was "a man of few words but to the point."

Motor Speedway on both two and four wheels, Baker thrilled fans—and frustrated lawmakers—with his daredevil transcontinental record runs onboard both motorcycles and automobiles. During an era when speed mattered more than safety when it came to attracting buyers for motorized transportation, nobody was faster than Cannon Ball Baker.

After years of eking out an existence in Weisburg, Baker and his family moved to Indianapolis in 1893 to try and better their meager standard of living. For a future automobile racer, Indianapolis turned out to be a great choice. Second only to Cleveland in the number of car manufacturers, Indianapolis had approximately sixty-five firms building automobiles over the years. At a young age Baker worked as an apprentice machinist at the Indianapolis Drop Forging Company for $3.50 per week. Saving his

sponsored a celebration at the local fairgrounds. Included in the day's events were several motorcycle races on an oval track. The contestants, from the Indianapolis Motorcycle Club, had earlier motored through downtown Crawfordsville in a parade. Eighteen riders then competed in various races. The first race was a five-mile dash for two-and-a-half to two-and-three-quarter horsepower machines. Baker, who finished second in a field of six, became hooked on the speed and thrill of the competition.

By 1909 Baker had competed in several motorcycle races in the Midwest, taking second and third place in a meet held in Columbus, Ohio, and winning three races at Troy, Ohio. Back in Indianapolis, the local racing community was excited about the announced summer opening of the Indianapolis Motor Speedway. Surprisingly, the first series of

Cannon Ball Baker stands next to the Indian motorcycle he used for his record-breaking San Diego to New York trip in May 1914. He later told Hoosier journalist Ernie Pyle that as a "skinny driver" he needed to sit on a sponge-rubber cushion he designed himself.

racing events to be held on the newly constructed oval was for motorcycles, not automobiles. Approximately 150 motorcycle riders from throughout the country competed in the planned two-day event, scheduled for August 14–15 and held under the auspices of the Federation of American Motorcyclists. To publicize the upcoming races, the *Indianapolis News* ran in its July 13 issue a large photograph of Baker on his Indian motorcycle under the caption "Daredevil Indianapolis Rider." This marked the first of several hundred photos of Baker to appear in papers and magazines throughout the country during the next forty years.

The Indianapolis Motor Speedway track, consisting of three sizes of crushed stone covered by pitch, had been completed only a few days before the races began. About ninety thousand wagonloads of stone were needed to cover the two-and-a-half-mile oval track, which was fifty feet wide on the straightaways and sixty feet wide on the turns. The motorcycle races were scheduled on this rough-paved surface—eight

of them on the first day and seven on the second. The races were to be from one to twenty-five miles in length and open to both amateurs and professionals. Baker signed up for twelve of the fifteen events.

On the first day of racing, during the fifth event, one of the top riders suffered serious injuries from a blown tire caused by the rough track. This unnerved many of the contestants, who withdrew their entries from later events. By the start of the seventh event, which was for the amateur championship over a ten-mile course, only four of the thirty entrants were willing to run the race. Baker took that chance and ended up winning the contest. Because of the few contestants remaining, FAM officials canceled the last race for the first day and all of the second day's events, maintaining—over the protests of Speedway officials—that the track was too dangerous for racing. The Speedway responded by paving the track with more than three million bricks that fall.

With his success at the Indianapolis race behind him, Baker continued to pursue his racing career. By

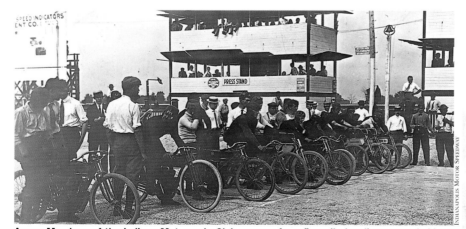

ABOVE: Members of the Indiana Motorcycle Club prepare for a five-mile handicap race, held as part of a planned two-day event in August 1909 at the new Indianapolis Motor Speedway. Baker (fourth from left) finished fourth in this race, but he did win the ten-mile Federation of American Motorcyclists' amateur championship. **RIGHT:** Labeled as a motorcycle rider possessing "great skill and nerve" by the *Indianapolis Star*, Baker insisted throughout his life that he was always "safety-minded whenever I drive."

INDIANAPOLIS MOTOR SPEEDWAY

INDIANAPOLIS MOTOR SPEEDWAY

Indianapolis Motor Speedway

A pair of motorcyclists zooms around the Indianapolis Motor Speedway racing oval during the ill-fated 1909 races at the racetrack. Local newspapers noted that police performed "excellent work" in keeping the excited crowds from rushing the track to see the accidents.

the end of 1912 he had accumulated 17,582 miles of motorcycle road racing, with 14,000 miles ridden in Cuba, Panama, and Jamaica. In addition, he had 1,583 miles of track racing to his credit. He came in first in fifty-three of the track races, second place in nine races, and third in eleven races, establishing eleven new speed records in the process.

From 1912 to 1924 Baker served as the factory representative for Indian motorcycles. During this early period of racing, he knew that in order to gain new speed records he had to break some speed laws. In 1913 the Indiana General Assembly passed laws limiting speed to ten miles per hour in villages and towns and twenty miles per hour on highways. Town marshals and county sheriffs were charged with enforcing the laws because there was no state police force at that time. Meanwhile, unmarked roads also presented another difficulty for Baker. The only signs were typically near towns where the roads were paved. There was no common name or numbering system for interstate, and in some cases intrastate, roads. Not until 1925 did officials establish a consistent national highway numbering system.

Perhaps the most challenging of all motorcycle contests Baker entered was a run from San Diego to New York City in 1914. The record time to beat was

twenty days, nine hours, and one minute established by Volney Davis of San Francisco two years earlier. Baker's gear included two extra innertubes, a short and long chain, a Graflex camera, a half-gallon canteen, and a .38-caliber revolver. The event was sanctioned by the FAM, and Baker had to report in by wire every night. This rule required him to plan his route through communities large enough to have telegraph facilities. The *Indianapolis News* carried a daily report of his progress from the start on May 3 to the finish on May 15. Of the 3,379 miles Baker drove, only four miles were on paved surfaces. At one point Baker rode on railroad ties for sixty-eight miles at night when the trains weren't running. He completed the trip in eleven days, eleven hours, and eleven minutes, which was nine days faster then the previous motorcycle record and four days faster than the fastest automobile, which had used a relay team of several drivers.

When Baker arrived in New York City, a newspaperman approached him and said, "Boy, you did a real job this time, so much so I am going to change your name." Baker said he replied that he already had enough nicknames, including "Demon," "Daredevil," "Fox," and "Warhorse." The reporter said, "None of these names are any good; you don't

On his 1915 cross-country automotive run onboard a Stutz from San Diego to New York, Baker used wooden planks to negotiate sand dunes near Yuma, Arizona. "Old Man Trouble doesn't run on schedule," Baker said, "and he doesn't set out any red lanterns for you. You've got always to be expecting the unexpected."

want any of them. Boy, I'm going to give you a real name, I'm going to call you 'Cannon Ball.'" Baker liked the name so well that he began to call himself that and later had the name copyrighted.

Much of the success of Baker's record run and many of his future runs was the meticulous route research he undertook before the start of each race. Before the first cross-country race, he and his wife spent two months compiling information on roads, bridges, and gasoline availability. In addition, Baker commissioned a friend to analyze weather records to determine the best possible starting date for a west to east coast run. Snow, rain, mud, wind, and hot temperatures had to be factored in since Baker, riding on a motorcycle, would be unprotected from the elements.

With his motorcycle reputation firmly established, Baker tried his hand at breaking the existing intercontinental automobile record. This opportunity came about through a 1915 meeting with the president of the Stutz Motor Car Company, which was headquartered in Indianapolis. Harry Stutz said to Baker, "Bake,

could you be as crazy on four wheels as you are on two? You drive it [the Bearcat], break the record, and the car is yours!" This was no small inducement as the Stutz retailed for $20,000. On the trip, Baker was accompanied by an observer, W. F. "Bill" Sturm, a no-nonsense *Indianapolis News* reporter. As an observer, Sturm recorded the details of the trip and secured the proper signatures at various checkpoints along the route. To alleviate any suspicion about who would be driving, Strum had the added qualification of not knowing how to drive. The fledgling American Automobile Association sanctioned, supervised, and authorized the race. This meant that the team had to check in every night at a specified destination to obtain the necessary signature by either the local railroad agent or postmaster.

Baker and Sturm left San Diego on May 7. Near Yuma, Arizona, the duo had to use two-by-six planks bolted together to navigate over sand dunes. At Dome, Arizona, they hired six Native Americans to pole the automobile across the Gila River. In New Mexico the Stutz became mired in quicksand in the middle of the Ruidoso River, a supposedly fordable watercourse. It took six horses five hours to free the automobile. The only other formidable barrier was the sea of mud encountered in the Midwest, but Baker's muscle and shovel together cleared the way. The pair finally arrived in New York City on May 18, 1915, in the record time of eleven days, seven hours, and fifteen minutes. Throughout the 3,728-mile trip, Baker and Sturm averaged four hours of sleep a night.

The next year, 1916, Baker and Sturm teamed up again to try to beat their own transcontinental record. This time Baker drove a Cadillac eight-cylinder standard roadster. The duo's luggage included an extra twenty-gallon gasoline tank, an ax and shovel, a two-gallon oil can, two desert water bags, fifty feet of rope, four air cushions, and a complete "pull-you-out," a device used to pull the car out of deep mud. Baker and Sturm started from Los Angeles at 12:01 a.m. on May 8 and encountered trouble by the time they

ABOVE, LEFT TO RIGHT: Baker's legendary skills as a driver earned for him a number of plum assignments, including serving as chief test pilot for a car named after World War I flying ace Eddie Rickenbacker (later owner of the Indianapolis Motor Speedway) and as driver for a five-thousand-mile endurance run for Columbia Motors's Tiger automobile. At right, Baker poses with the two-ton General Motors truck he drove cross country in 1927.
BOTTOM: Horsepower of a different kind aids Baker in crossing the Ruidoso River in New Mexico during a 1915 intercontinental trip.

reached the Mojave Desert. An pipe leading to an oil line broke, leaving them stranded. Baker walked along a nearby railroad track in the 120-degree heat to search for help. Five miles later he found a small railroad station where he flagged down the next train. Because the train carried no spare oil, he hopped aboard in hopes of finding oil at the next station. As the train approached the spot where the car was stalled, however, Baker noticed that another car was there as well. Baker jumped off the train and learned that Sturm had talked the driver of the other car into "lending" them a gallon of oil. This was accomplished by draining oil from the other car's crankcase into an emptied water bag and then into the Cadillac.

The next major problem was mud, especially in Missouri where at one place it took two hours to drive ten miles. A short distance later the car skidded into a deep ditch, even though the tires had chains installed. It took three hours with the aid of four mules and a block and tackle to pull out the car. The remainder of the trip was relatively uneventful, with Baker and Sturm arriving in New York City on May 15. The new record of seven days, eleven hours, and fifty-three minutes eclipsed their previous year's record by about four days.

One event during the trip had long-term ramifications for future races—Baker received his first speeding ticket. In Collinsville, Illinois, a motorcycle policeman pulled Baker over, arrested him for driving thirty-two miles per hour, and took him to the

LEFT: Riding his beloved Indian motorcycle, Baker negotiates some tough terrain in the Mojave Desert during a 1919 long-distance run. As roadways were improved in America, Baker predicted that drivers would "drive faster and faster, just as sure as a man who owns a shotgun is going to go hunting the first chance he gets." RIGHT: At the 1922 Indianapolis 500, Baker, accompanied by mechanic Shorty Hanson, finished in eleventh place for Louis Chevrolet's Frontenac racing team. Jimmy Murphy won the race that year driving a Duesenberg.

police station. Baker appeared in front of a judge, pleaded guilty, was fined $3.60 plus $5.00 in court costs, and was let go, all in the space of twenty minutes. As Baker's fame and reputation for fast driving increased, so did the desire of many police agencies to arrest him for speeding. In the future, to avoid known speed traps, Baker bypassed cities and headed across open country.

During the rest of 1916 and 1917, Baker went back to his first love, the Indian motorcycle. He rode in Australia, where he set many speed and endurance records on a special road racecourse. In August 1917 he established twelve- and twenty-four-hour records on the board speedway at Cincinnati. With the advent of World War I, however, racing activities were curtailed at the request of the federal government. Too old to serve in the military, Baker was "drafted" along with other celebrities to lead bond drives. In addition, when not on tour, Baker taught draftees how to drive automobiles at Indianapolis's Fort Benjamin Harrison.

Perhaps because of the war, the focus of automobile marketing turned from speed to reliability and economy. When the conflict ended, Baker once again took to the road, this time to visit all forty-eight state capitals. The automobile of choice was the Revere, made in Logansport, Indiana. Baker left Indianapolis on June 12, 1918, and reached his final destination of Frankfort, Kentucky, on September 13. He had driven 16,234 miles in seventy-seven days, eighteen hours, and fifteen minutes. For a while the results of the endurance run boosted public interest in the fledgling automobile manufacturer, but by 1926 the Revere joined many other car makes on the scrapheap.

Hoping to win valuable publicity, several automobile manufacturers competed in 1920 to capture the record for the coast to coast run. One of these firms was the Templar Motors Corporation of Cleveland, Ohio, who hired Baker as a driver. In June, as a warm-up for the big event, Baker drove a Templar from New York City to Chicago. He made the 922-mile run in twenty-six hours and fifty minutes, never turning off the engine. In July, Baker, accompanied by Arthur Holliday, a Templar mechanic, drove the same car from New York to Los Angeles in six days, seventeen hours, and thirty-three minutes. Baker had to weld steel plates to the car's undercarriage to prevent engine damage from rocks while crossing Arizona. His total sleep for the trip was seventeen hours.

Once again Baker received a speeding ticket. He was clocked driving forty-five miles per hour in a fifteen mile per hour zone in a San Bernardino, California, speed trap. Commenting on Baker's arrest for speeding, Charles J. Chenu, the superintendent of the California Motor Vehicle Department, stated publicly, "There is to be no violation of the California Motor Vehicle Act. As long as that law says the speed limit is 35 miles an hour, and that only where the road is straight and unobstructed, as far as I and my inspectors can do it, we will see there is no car making faster time." Apparently Baker wasn't listening because just a few months later he again traversed California in a record run on his motorcycle. This time he went south to north from Tijuana, Mexico, to the Canadian border, establishing a new record of two days and five hours, beating his old record by thirteen hours.

In 1922 Baker hit the big time. Louis Chevrolet asked him to join the Frontenac race team in running at the Indianapolis 500. Baker qualified for the sixteenth starting position with an average speed of ninety miles per hour. Unfortunately, because of a faulty ignition and other mishaps, he never had a real chance to win. He managed to move up to eleventh position by the end of the race, but that left him out of the money. He never raced in the Indianapolis 500 again, but he continued to test-drive various cars at the track over the years. By his own estimate he had driven 48,000 miles at the Indianapolis oval by the time he hung up his racing gloves.

From May to August 1923 Baker established several speed and economy records as the chief test-driver for the Indianapolis-built Cole automobile. He logged 8,000 miles in several Midwestern states, averaging between fifteen and twenty miles per gallon on various runs. This performance was impressive enough for Cole to take out large newspaper display advertisements touting the economy and reliability of its car. Hassler shock absorbers of Indianapolis also featured Baker in ads touting its product, which was used on the Cole. The ad stated: "Baker had driven 500,000 miles, 20 times the distance around the earth—an average of 82 miles a day for his 17 years of record breaking runs."

In 1926 Baker turned his back on the high-powered and expensive cars he usually selected for his cross-country runs. This time he broke his previous record driving an ordinary Model T Roadster. He made the run from New York to Los Angeles in five days, two hours, and thirteen minutes. Baker's record prompted a telegram from Henry Ford himself, who said, "Congratulations, wonderful run." In recalling the telegram with a reporter, Baker laughingly said that Ford was "a man of few words but to the point."

Never one to turn down a proposal, Baker drove a General Motors truck, loaded with three tons of Atlantic Ocean water, to a new cross-country record in September 1927. Upon Baker's arrival in San Francisco in five days, seventeen hours, and thirty-six minutes, he was the guest of honor at a city hall reception. Later he joined a parade through the business section of the city and then drove the truck down to the nearest beach, where he ceremoniously dumped the contents into the Pacific Ocean. He had slept only four hours during the five-day run, quite a feat for the forty-five-year-old driver.

One of Baker's most successful relationships with an automobile and its manufacturer came in 1928 and 1929. In July 1928 he signed a two-year contract with the Franklin Automobile Company to show what the air-cooled car could do in the race game. Baker had won the executives over with a proposal that was succinct and to the point: "No record. No pay." As expected, though, Baker established many new records with the car, including one for a round-trip run between New York and Los Angeles, completed in sixty-nine hours and thirty-one minutes, with all timing checked by Western Union. Baker also drove the air-cooled Franklin on other record-breaking runs, including trips up Mount Washington, Lookout

LEFT: John Willys, president of Willy-Overland, Inc., shakes hands with Baker before the driver's departure from New York in 1926. Baker took a stock Overland Whippet on a cross-country run to San Diego under the supervision of the Automobile Association of America. **MIDDLE:** A crowd at a Western Union station in San Francisco cheers Baker's cross-country drive onboard a Ford Model T Roadster Runabout in 1926. For his run, Baker had agreements with twenty-three equipment manufacturers. **RIGHT:** A grizzled Baker at the end of his last intercontinental motorcycle run in 1941 at age fifty-nine.

Mountain, and Pikes Peak, as well as many intercity courses throughout the country. His final run with a Franklin came in May 1930, when he drove from Indianapolis to French Lick at a record breaking speed of sixty-six miles per hour.

In 1928 a long article, titled "Speed Ads Soft Pedaled," appeared in *Motor Age*, an important trade publication. Much criticism had been leveled at automobile manufacturers for glorifying speed in their advertisements, so automotive industry executives met to discuss the matter. Many defended their actions. H. C. Hersh, Auburn Automobile Company advertising manager, said, "We do not sell speed when we advertise the breaking of stock car records. It is unlawful to drive as fast as 100 m.p.h. Neither does the public want to average 84 m.p.h. for 24 hours, but the ability of a car to travel 100 m.p.h. or average 84 m.p.h. for 24 hours proves endurance and value."

No matter what automotive manufacturers said in defense of using speed to sell cars, however, the handwriting was on the wall. Public pressure for increased road safety, enforceable with the establishment of state police departments, including Indiana's in 1933, would soon put an end to long-distance speed runs, and race drivers had to look to other competitive venues to promote automobiles. For Baker, this turn

of events could not have come at a worse time. His only son had just died unexpectedly at the age of fifteen from an infected tooth. This was a severe blow to both Baker and his wife, Elenora, leading to an extended period of mourning. With the encouragement of friends, however, Baker soon took the road again, ignoring the criticism directed at speed merchants and setting records in the air-cooled Franklin.

In 1930 Baker again teamed up with Stutz for another transcontinental run, fifteen years after his first record run with the company. This time he made the trip in a record-breaking sixty hours and fifty-one minutes. The next year, looking for new roads to conquer, Baker test-drove the legendary Franklin V-12 prototype at Daytona Beach, Florida. In 1933 he set new records at Mount Wilson, California, and at Mount Washington, New Hampshire, driving a Graham Eight. His final attempt to break the transcontinental speed record came in the spring of 1933. Driving a supercharged Graham, he made the trip in fifty-three hours and thirty minutes. Baker said the thirty minutes was the only rest he got. This record has never officially been broken for a one-man crossing.

At the age of fifty-one, Baker believed it was time to travel another road. As he noted, "Traffic was getting too thick and increasing speed laws and police made

LEFT TO RIGHT: At the end of his career, Baker tinkered with inventions, including a combination carburetor and manifold, reminisced about his long career, and posed with *Gunsmoke* actor James Arness at a 1958 race at the Darlington Speedway as part of his work as commissioner of the National Association for Stock Car Auto Racing.

the glamorous transcontinental record a thing of the past, but it had served its purpose." He had driven more than 3.5 million miles by this time and had never had a collision with another vehicle, much less scratched a fender. So instead of speeding across the country, he spent much of 1933 on a "safety tour" of the nation, accompanied by Robert C. Graham, vice president of the Graham-Paige Motors Corporation.

In the latter part of the 1930s and early 1940s, Baker spent much of his time at his home workshop, located across the street from Indianapolis's Garfield Park. He invented a device he said would enable automobiles to travel fifty miles on a gallon of gasoline. This combination carburetor and manifold was to sell for $10. Baker actually received a patent for his "Gas Engine Fuel Economizer" in November 1943, but the invention never became a commercial success. During this period he also worked on improving the old rotary valve engine, making it suitable for a one-cylinder motorcycle. In 1941, wishing to test the results of his labors, Baker jumped on one of his modified motorcycles and drove it across the country from Los Angeles to New York in six days, six hours, and twenty-five minutes. It was to be the last of his 126 transcontinental runs.

Perhaps the greatest tribute to Baker's legendary driving skills came when officials of the fledgling National Association for Stock Car Auto Racing asked

him in 1947 to be the organization's first commissioner. He gladly accepted and was active in managing NASCAR until his death. Even after being appointed commissioner, Baker had to try his hand at breaking automobile records. Between 1947 and 1949, he broke two hill-climbing and two economy-run records with a Nash 600 series and a Nash Ambassador. He completed his last recorded professional driving assignment in 1952 for a Willys economy run.

Until his death on May 10, 1960, Cannon Ball continued his work for NASCAR and made appearances at numerous racetracks around the nation. Baker's name and exploits have been enshrined in many venues, including the Motorsports Hall of Fame at Novi, Michigan, and the Motorcycle Hall of Fame at Pickerington, Ohio, where the restored Indian that won one of the first Indianapolis Motor Speedway races in 1909 is on display. Baker's gravestone at Indianapolis's Crown Hill Cemetery is simply inscribed "Cannon Ball Baker." It should have included an epitaph declaring him the greatest stock-car driver that ever lived.

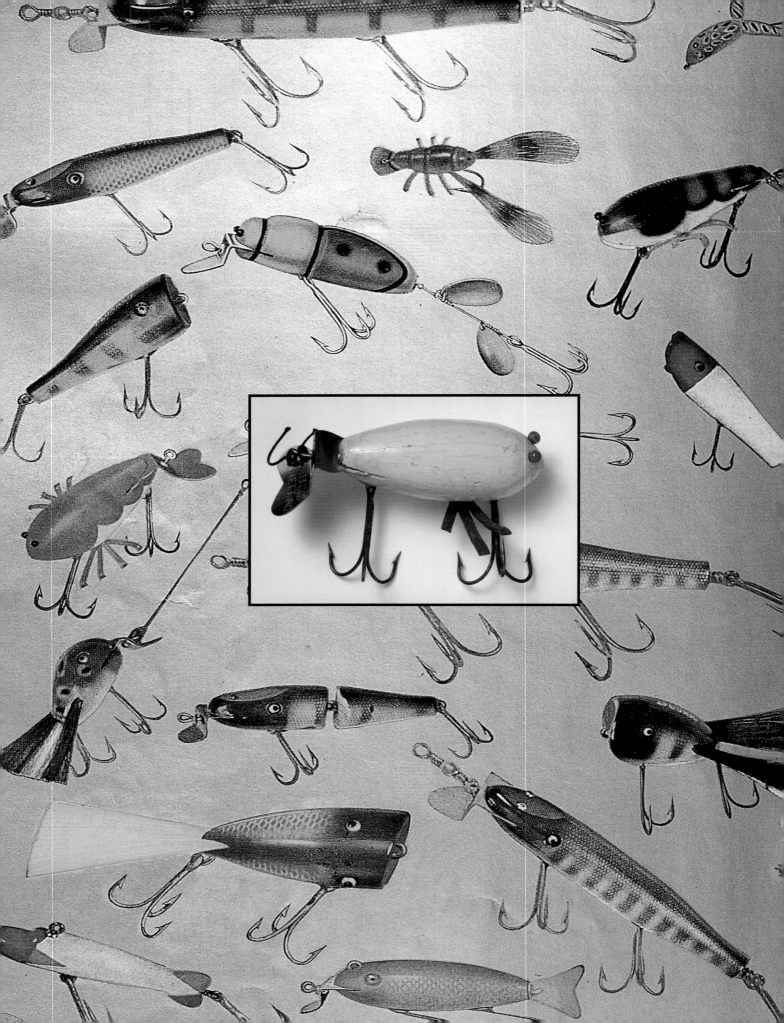

A Lure for All Seasons

The Creek Chub Bait Company of Garrett, Indiana

Rachel S. Roberts

ALL ARTIFACTS COURTESY STEVE PEPPLE; PHOTOGRAPHS BY DALE BERNSTEIN

When rummaging through attics,

garages, or other places where junk tends to gather, keep your eyes open. If you find a fishing lure with the tiny initials C.C.B.CO. stamped on its stainless steel lip, you may have found a treasure. Today lures once produced by the Creek Chub Bait Company, as well as the company's old catalogs, advertisements, posters, calendars, and miscellaneous items, are coveted by collectors and antique dealers. Even a small lure that at one time cost less than fifty cents can now command a handsome price.

From the inception of the Creek Chub Bait Company in Garrett, Indiana, "the handcrafted, painted lures were magic," said Sam Miller, a Creek Chub enthusiast. Not only were the lures beautiful works of art, but they also worked exceptionally well. This combination of form and function is part of what makes the lures so attractive. Also appealing, according to Miller, is the history of the company itself, with its elements of American inventiveness and entrepreneurship.

The company's story begins with a trio of friends. Henry S. Dills, George M. Schulthess, and Carl H. Heinzerling were fishing buddies who lived in the DeKalb County town of Garrett. Heinzerling and Schulthess owned adjacent cottages on Lake Wawasee in nearby Kosciusko County, and Dills, a clerk for the Baltimore and Ohio Railroad, often visited his friends there. The men shared lures, compared how they worked, and discussed how they could be improved. Sometimes Dills demonstrated to his friends lures he had created himself.

Even as a young man Dills was interested in making lures; he whittled tiny pieces of wood and took notes on how his creations performed. Very few artificial lures were available at the time, and most fishermen used in-line spinners or live bait. Intrigued, Dills experimented with wooden lures and developed a wiggling fish concept that he believed would be marketable.

Local legend states that on one of his visits to Lake Wawasee, Dills discussed with Schulthess the idea of

Packed in this old tackle box are several Creek Chub lures. A #106 Wiggler in goldfish hangs along the side.

starting a company to manufacture the artificial lures and that by the end of the visit Heinzerling also had signed on. Other historians claim that Dills first peddled his ideas to established manufacturers and that he did not join with Schulthess and Heinzerling until much later. Whatever the exact beginnings, it was a good partnership. Dills possessed the artistic flair and interest in designing lures, and both Heinzerling and Schulthess had capital and considerable business experience. Heinzerling owned a Garrett hardware store, a successful enterprise he ran until his death in 1950. Schulthess had interests in real estate, manufacturing, restaurants and taverns, and farming. He was also involved in politics and served four terms as Garrett's mayor.

The men decided to name their new company for the creek chub, a type of minnow found in surrounding waterways. Although historians dispute in what year they began manufacturing their lures (many sources, including a commemorative plaque in Garrett, indicate it was 1906, while more reliable documentation seems to indicate the three partners didn't join forces until 1916), one thing is certain: in the beginning the new Creek Chub Bait Company was very small—"not much more than an overblown garage operation," according to Gretel Smith, Heinzerling's granddaughter.

The company started producing its first lure, the Wiggler, in Schulthess's basement on South Franklin Street in Garrett. When twenty or thirty lures were ready to be sold, Dills took them to hardware dealers in Fort Wayne. It is also said that as Dills demonstrated the lures to fellow travelers on the interurban, he often sold out his stock. The demand for lures was so great that the owners expanded the line and moved production to a house owned by Schulthess on the corner of Cowen and Keyser Streets. At first the men assembled their lures in the evening, and a lone female employee continued the work by day. Before long, however, the workforce grew to eight employees. As the company prospered, it added secretaries, clerks, and salesmen to the payroll until eventually as many as eighty employees were involved in manufacturing, shipping, and selling lures.

In 1918 the Creek Chub Bait Company was incorporated, and production soon moved to the Garrett Hotel Annex, located at 113–117 East Keyser Street, where it was later enlarged. One resident recalled that it was "in a nondescript building with green

Most sources claim that the Georgia fisherman who caught the world-record twenty-two-pound, four-ounce largemouth bass in 1932 used a #2401 Wigglefish in perch scale.

doors, and I remember when I went by there on my way home from school, it always smelled like lacquer."

During the Great Depression, when other companies were closing and laying off employees, Creek Chub added a second shift. The people who worked at the firm generally lived within walking distance. The company was conveniently located near grocery stores, the bakery, the drugstore, the doctor, and, of course, Heinzerling's hardware store.

Most Creek Chub employees were women. The reason for this, one Garrett resident explained, was the fact that "the work was delicate and women have nimble fingers." Still, Creek Chub was a man's business, with perks for the male workers. "If a male employee wanted a fishing lure, he could take one home," said former worker Mel Diederich. "But if a woman wanted one, she had to pay twenty-five cents for it." Explaining this injustice in light of modern times, Diederich said, "If the man were to take a lure home, it meant he would be using it to go fishing. If a woman took it, most likely she would sell it or give it away." Despite some of the preferences shown to their male counterparts, women nevertheless seemed to enjoy working at Creek Chub. Old photographs show smiling employees at annual picnics and swimming outings at Hamilton Lake. The company even sponsored a women's basketball team.

Creek Chub was not without its labor problems, however, and workers went on strike in September 1941. When the seventeen-day affair was settled, final concessions included recognizing a union as the sole bargaining unit, settling future disputes by arbitration without work stoppages, establishing seniority rights, increasing hourly and piecework rates, and adjusting overtime and leaves of absence with no discrimination against striking employees when they returned to work. By the mid-1940s the company offered an average wage of nineteen dollars a week. To meet the growing demand for its products, Creek Chub opened in 1942 a second plant in Ashley, Indiana, eighteen miles north of Garrett. Many of

C.C.B.CO. LURE

The Creek Chub Bait Co.

GARRETT INDIANA

4TH ANNUAL
Antique Fishing Lures and Collectibles Show

SATURDAY, NOVEMBER 24, 2001
American Legion - Garrett, Indiana

#3850 BEETLE
Invented By Gordon S. Dills

Gordon S. Dills

the company's employees worked out of the Ashley plant, preparing the bodies of the lures and applying primer, until operations moved to a new plant on Quincy Street in Garrett in 1957.

As Creek Chub pointed out in its promotions, one of the fundamental selling points for its lures was quality—quality of wood, paint, design, and time. A 1933 catalog, for example, offered a convincing description of its wares, promising "genuine cedar bodies in all floating lures—no pine or basswood" and "extra high finish on all nickeled parts." "We do our own plating and polishing and do it right," the catalog guaranteed. The company placed great importance in the materials it used and the craftsmanship of its employees, and such care is part of the reason the lures were popular then and remain so today.

Selection of wood was especially important. White cedar, which for years was plentiful, was the main wood used in the production of Creek Chub lures. White cedar is light, floats well, and is easily turned on a lathe. Moreover, it doesn't shrink when paint is applied to it. The company had an exclusive process of treating the wood to prevent the finish from cracking or scaling. Auburn contractor Cal Grosscup, who also made baseball bats, fishing poles, and rolling pins, as well as wooden shipping boxes for General Electric, did wood-turning work for Creek Chub for four years. "I had to find a source for the light wood they used," he said. "Finally I found a man in Michigan who could sell me some." Creek Chub also obtained white cedar from Minnesota. During the 1960s, when white cedar was hard to find, Canadian basswood served as a substitute. Some lures were also made of plastic, but after a new source of white cedar was located, the company went back to using wood. The work kept Grosscup busy. "We had to follow certain specifications," he said. "I kept six lathes going. Each lathe cost around six or seven thousand dollars, and we turned out two or three thousand [lures] a day."

ABOVE: Creek Chub's employees gather outside the company's factory in Garrett, circa 1925. At far right in the second row is Henry S. Dills. The first two men in the back row are Gordon S. Dills, Henry's son, and George M. Schulthess. OPPOSITE: A limited-edition poster advertises the 2001 Creek Chub reunion and collectibles show. The poster features Gordon S. Dills, who served as president of the company from 1945 to 1958.

Although Grosscup produced the wooden lures in record numbers, it took time to paint them and add the hardware. One element that contributed to the quality and beauty of the lures was the fact that Creek Chub always used the best paint available. Employees applied either cream or black primer then painted the designs by hand. The painted details included variations of lines, flecks, dots, and colors. In 1918 Dills invented and patented a spray-painted scale pattern that entailed spray painting through netting, which gave a luminous quality to the lure. Employees used other painting techniques as well, including dipping. After the paint dried, they dipped the lures in lacquer several times and allowed it to harden. The lacquer gave the lures a hard-gloss, shiny, protective coating. By the time the lures were ready to be shipped, they had as many as fourteen coats of primer, paint, and lacquer.

June 19 - 1926

Members of the Creek Chub family enjoy themselves at the company's eighth-annual employee picnic, held at Hamilton Lake in Steuben County on June 19, 1926.

In the early days of production, color choices were few. By 1924, however, the company had expanded its offerings to more than twenty. As the selection of colors continued to grow over the decades, the standardization of numbers eventually became necessary. In his *Collector's Encyclopedia of Creek Chub Lures and Collectibles*, author Harold Smith (with valuable help from Derek Heinzerling, grandson of company cofounder Carl Heinzerling) presents pages of lure numbers and color numbers for quick reference.

The painted lures are simply beautiful. The #909 Baby Pikie in brilliant greenback, for example, has gold coloring under a green scale, a rather rare pattern. Equally interesting is the #3900 Sucker, offered in yellow and black. The patterns and designs of the lures are too numerous to list, but each is exquisite. Whether painted with the #15 tan crab color, the #19 frog color, the #06 goldfish color, or the #31 rainbow fire color, a Creek Chub lure continues to hold strong appeal.

In addition to its wide selection of standard lures, Creek Chub offered custom designs. Carl Heinzerling's son Harry, for example, developed a special lure for Ed Grisa, a friend and Wisconsin fishing guide who wanted a lure that would imitate whitefish and cisco. After two years of testing colors, Harry came up with the #44 whitefish pattern in 1974. Others learned of the successful new pattern and began requesting it so much that the company added the color to its chart the next year. Austin "Toad" Van Houton, a Creek Chub plant manager, also created unique products and hardware. He hand-turned for a customer in upstate New York a large lure known as the Chautauqua Special, and he created for the #200 Baby Wiggler and other lures an inventive painted lip, now known as the Toad Van Houton lip.

Creek Chub outfitted its standard lures with lips manufactured by a variety of companies across the country. The earliest lures bore no name on their lips. "In 1917 or 1918," however, wrote Smith, "lips were introduced that had the name 'CCBCO, Garrett, Ind.' stamped on them." After Creek Chub patented its lip in 1920, it became general practice to include that patent date on all the lips. (New collectors often mistake this for the manufacture date, which is not the case: lures made as late as 1978 had the 1920 patent date stamped on their lips.) By the time the Pikie was produced in 1921, standard lips were in common use. Though custom-made lures often featured painted lips, "standard lips were never painted in production lures," said Smith. A reinforced lip utilizing two vertical ribs for strength became the standard lip for all larger baits in 1935, and in 1950 the company introduced a deep-diving lip.

The methods by which the hooks are attached to lures help collectors date some Creek Chub lures and differentiate them from those made by other manufacturers. Throughout its years of production, Creek Chub attached hooks to the body of a lure by using screws with eyes. To keep water from seeping into the body, the company first placed a washer at the base of each screw, but it soon replaced the washer with a tiny shallow cup inserted into the body, allowing the hook to ride against the body so the bait would appear more lifelike. Over the years, the shallow cups gave way to deeper ones. It is important to note that authentic Creek Chub lures do not have painted cups.

Other features also help distinguish Creek Chub lures. The use of spinners or propellers began in 1924 with the #1500 Injured Minnow design. "The spinner is easily identified by the hyphen-like reinforcement on each side of the center hole," noted Smith. Creek Chub most often applied glass taxidermy eyes to its lures, though it did use an airbrush to paint eyes on some of them. To combat the growing cost of glass eyes, in the 1960s the company began applying tack eyes and painting them. Finally, in 1935 Creek Chub began labeling its lures. From 1935 to 1950 it used a military-style stenciling, from 1950 to 1964 it used a gold-embossed pressed stamp, and from 1964 to 1978 it used gold-foil labels. Sometimes the lures were labeled with the name of the company, sometimes with the name of the design, and sometimes with a combination of the two. Many times, however, lures received no labels at all.

In the 1920s the company made eight different fly-fishing baits in thirty-seven patterns and colors. These included tiny lures, such as the Creek Bug Wiggler and the Fly Rod Pikie, and more typical flies, such as the Bass Fly and the Hopper Fly. Some of the tiny lures were successful enough to merit twenty years of production, but the flies were produced for only two years and are now extremely rare.

Creek Chub prided itself on its quality and innovation, and as part of its efforts it developed and tested many prototype lures. The process was often long and tedious, however, taking between two and five years. Because of the difficulties involved, the company seldom introduced completely new lures, though it did so on occasion. More commonly it directed its efforts toward modifying and improving existing lures.

When the company did produce a new or modified lure, it focused upon finding a suitable name. Coming up with the name was not a capricious matter, although some names do reflect lighthearted times. The Dingbat, for example, received its moniker when

plant manager Austin Van Houton and fellow coworkers gathered at a bar and decided to name it for Earl "Dingbat" Weaver, who was dating Van Houton's sister. On a more serious note, the Victory Bomber lure was named to honor World War II troops. It featured on its sides the letter *V* and a dot-dot-dot-dash (the Morse Code symbol for *V*). One Pikie was named for President Dwight D. Eisenhower. It was red, white, and blue and featured five stars. Incidentally, during the war the #5000 Close Pin was included in many navy survival kits.

According to historians and residents who worked at Creek Chub, the success of the company owed much to its superb marketing. The firm invested significantly in promotion and by the 1930s was spending as much as $25,000 to $30,000 a year for catalogs and advertisements with photographs and detailed descriptions of its products. One employee noted that the company maintained a mailing list with 75,000 names. Packaging was also an important part of Creek Chub's marketing. In the early days the

Creek Chub's first lure was the #100 Wiggler, shown here with its original box. Like the lures they used to hold, the company's early boxes are also popular with today's collectors. In 1999 a buyer paid $1,400 for one of them.

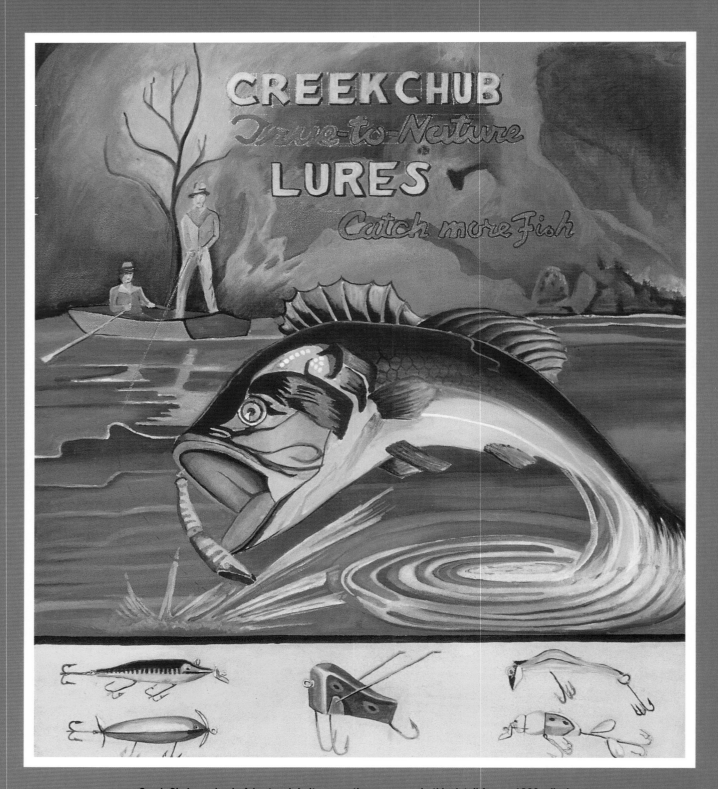

Creek Chub used colorful artwork in its promotions, as seen in this detail from a 1930s display.

company packed its lures in plain boxes made of yellow cardboard with black printing, but later it used boxes and shipping cartons that were more visually appealing, with color print and illustrations. The business's promotional efforts paid off: by the mid-1940s Creek Chub shipped its lures to every state and at least thirty-nine foreign countries.

Of course all the effort Creek Chub put into manufacturing and marketing its lures would have been futile if the lures did not perform up to expectations. This was not the case. Indeed, many testimonials indicate just how effective Creek Chub lures were. "It was simple," one fisherman said of their appeal. "They caught fish." In 1967 Harry Heinzerling, who managed the company after his father Carl's death, wrote, "It's a lot of fun to fish with a Pikie, the jointed model, especially. As it comes through the water, you'll get the feeling you're getting your money's worth. Maybe it's the way it shimmies through the water with that back hook, giving the impression of fast, tail action." Steve Pepple, an avid collector who many consider to be Creek Chub's unofficial historian, said that Harry Truman regularly ordered lures while in the White House and that he reported to company officials that "that Crawdad is a damned good bait." Legend also says that singer Bing Crosby was a happy customer, once refusing to go fishing in Spain until he received his special order.

Although methods of keeping records and tracking publicity weren't sophisticated in the early days, Creek Chub catalogs do include impressive letters and pictures of customers extolling the virtues of their Creek Chub baits. In 1924, for example, a Creek Chub #700 Pikie caught a twenty-pound, two-ounce largemouth bass in Florida. In 1932 a Georgia fisherman used a #2401 Wigglefish in perch scale (or according to some sources the #2100 Fintail

#3800 Beetle lures are shown here in one of Creek Chub's shipping boxes. This box holds a dozen individually packaged lures.

Shiner) to catch a twenty-two-pound, four-ounce largemouth bass, a world record that still stands. In 1941 a #700 Pikie snagged a world-record smallmouth bass that weighed twelve pounds, nine ounces. For three years #2000 Creek Darters caught the largest black bass in America on artificial lures. And in 1952 a #3200 Plunker on an eight-pound test line caught a forty-four-pound barracuda in the Bahamas.

It is common knowledge that fishermen exaggerate and tell great stories, but enough facts and pictures exist to substantiate that many world records were garnered by fishermen using Creek Chub lures—records such as the fifty-eight-pound, four-ounce muskellunge caught in Ontario, the eighteen-pound walleye caught in Wisconsin, the sixty-six-pound striped bass caught off the coast of Connecticut, and the thirty-six-pound snook caught in Costa Rica.

The Creek Chub Bait Company remained an Indiana fixture until the late 1970s. In 1978, with declining sales, increased competition, and other challenges facing them, surviving members of the Heinzerling and Schulthess families decided to sell the company to the Lazy Ike Corporation of Iowa. That fall production began again in Garrett. Optimism was high, but sales were dismal. In 1979 Lazy Ike shut down the Garrett plant, and the business soon went bankrupt. In the ensuing years a succession of firms bought the Creek Chub patents, and today an Arkansas-based company, Pradco, owns the Creek Chub name and manufactures lures under it. Though Creek Chub's days in its hometown are long gone, many people in Garrett still take a strong interest in it. A plaque now marks the site where the firm was founded, and for many years the city has hosted a Creek Chub festival and reunion for former employees.

The passion for Creek Chub also lives on in collectors of antique lures. According to the National Fishing Lure Collectors Club, there are more than seven thousand recognized collectors of specific lures or memorabilia. Many of these focus only on Creek Chub products. It is easy to understand why. The Creek Chub lures are beautiful and classic, and their names, whether Mitie Mouse, Silver Sides, River Rustler, Pocket Rocket, Bull Pup, Wicked Wiggler, or Sinful Sal, add a certain mystique and charm to collecting.

Once people learn about the quality and legendary beauty of Creek Chub Bait Company fishing lures, many are eager to search through barns, sheds, tackle boxes, and toolboxes in hopes of finding one or perhaps even a discarded Creek Chub box caught under a tangle of fish line. Whether it is a River Scamp or a common Pikie, finding a Creek Chub lure is exciting. As Sam Miller said, "They're pure magic." Perhaps that as much as anything explains why fishermen and collectors appreciate their value, as do artists, craftspeople, and antique dealers.

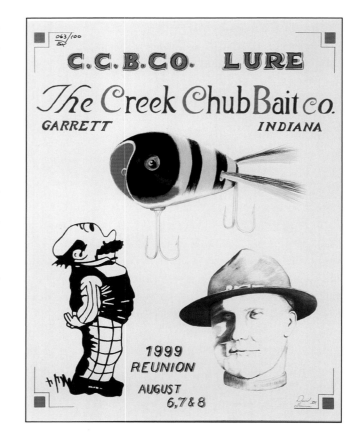

CHARLES STAHL,
RIGHTFIELDER, BOSTON, 1899.

Requiem for a Ballplayer

Indiana's Chick Stahl
Pete Cava

A lucky few get to retire, but sooner or later almost all baseball managers are fired. It happened to Leo Durocher and Casey Stengel, and both are in the National Baseball Hall of Fame. Billy Martin managed five different teams and was fired by each of them—five times by the New York Yankees alone. In major-league history, however, only one manager's career ended in suicide. The tragedy took place ninety-seven years ago in West Baden Springs, Indiana, when Boston Red Sox skipper Chick Stahl took his own life two weeks prior to the start of the 1907 season.

Technically, Charles Sylvester "Chick" Stahl had resigned as manager three days before his death. Stahl's decision to terminate his managerial career—and then his life—was apparently part of a series of events that doomed the seemingly carefree athlete. Born on January 10, 1873, in the northeastern Indiana town of Avilla, Stahl grew up approximately twenty miles to the south in Fort Wayne. The husky, handsome youngster starred for a local semipro club, the Pilseners, and in 1894 went off to play professionally for Battle Creek in the Michigan League. The Boston Beaneaters (today's Atlanta Braves) drafted Stahl after the 1896 season when he hit .337 for Buffalo in the Eastern League.

In his first big-league season Stahl hit .354 as the right fielder for the pennant-winning Beaneaters. After Boston won a second National League title in 1898 (with Stahl batting .308), a correspondent for the *Sporting News* promised a "right hearty welcome" when Stahl returned to Fort Wayne for the off-season.

Described as a quiet but enthusiastic player, the five-foot-ten-inch, 160-pound Stahl spent two more years with the Beaneaters. When the American League became a major circuit in 1901, he moved across town to play for the Boston Somersets, a team that eventually became the Red Sox. Another Beaneaters player who changed uniforms was Jimmy Collins, Stahl's close friend. Considered the best third baseman of the era, Collins became the Somersets' manager. With

(vertical, right margin) COURTESY THE PRINT DEPARTMENT, MCGREEVEY COLLECTION, BOSTON PUBLIC LIBRARY

Often touted as a potential Hall of Fame player, Chick Stahl had a .307 career batting average and led the league in triples in 1904.

his buddy Stahl playing center field, Collins guided the Somersets to a second-place finish in the 1901 season. By now Stahl was Fort Wayne's greatest sports celebrity, as well as one of baseball's most popular players—the Larry Bird of his era. When Boston visited Fort Wayne for a regular-season game with Cleveland on August 31, 1902, Stahl's adoring fans presented him with a gold-handled cane and three floral arrangements.

Troubled by an abscess early in 1903, Stahl sat out almost half the season. He dropped twenty pounds, and his batting average dipped to just .274—forty-nine points below his 1902 average. "Stahl looks like a very sick man," reported the *Sporting News* on June 27, 1903. "He has lost much flesh and has bad color, but the doctor says good nursing will bring him around all right." Boston finished in first place that year and challenged Pittsburgh, the National League champions, to a World Series, the first-ever post-season meeting between the two leagues' pennant winners.

Elected to the National Baseball Hall of Fame by a veteran's committee in 1945, Jimmy Collins has been called by many experts one of the game's greatest third basemen. Collins batted .346 in 1897 and led the National League in home runs the next year with fifteen.

Recovered in time to play in the Series, Stahl led his team with a .303 average and ten hits as the Somersets whipped the Pirates five games to three in a best-of-nine matchup. When Boston (by now called the Pilgrims) again won the pennant in 1904, the National League champion New York Giants, wary of the Pirates' fate a year earlier, refused to play them.

The Pilgrims were sold in 1904 to twenty-nine-year-old John I. Taylor, whose father owned the *Boston Globe*. When Taylor cut player salaries after the 1905 season, the weekly paper *Sporting Life* reported a "serious clash" between the owner and manager Collins. Following intervention by American League officials, *Sporting Life* reported in February 1906 that Collins would "have full charge of all matters concerning the players." The agreement worked fine on paper. Taylor continued to meddle, however, frequently berating the players after a loss. Late in the 1906 season, with the Pilgrims stumbling in last place, Collins resigned as manager and Stahl replaced him on an interim basis. Boston finished last in the league with 49 wins and 105 losses, including 26 losses in 40 games with Stahl at the helm.

Rumors abounded during the off-season. *Sporting Life* said Taylor wanted Stahl to take the managerial reins on a permanent basis but that the Hoosier native would not accept the job without the blessing of his friend Collins. In October the newspaper hinted that the thirty-three-year-old Stahl might be getting married. "'Tis said that Chick contemplates matrimony," quipped the October 20, 1906, edition. "'Bout time." The news surprised Stahl's teammates, who had heard him declare that he would never marry while he was still an active player. Yet on November 14, 1906, Stahl married Julia Harmon in her hometown of Roxbury, Massachusetts, not far from the team's ballpark at the Huntington Avenue Grounds. The newlyweds honeymooned in Hot Springs, Arkansas, and passed through Buffalo, New York, on the return trip to visit Collins.

Stahl was unsure about taking his old friend's job. "I would make a nice manager," he once scoffed.

"Why, I couldn't release a man even if he was no good at all." Prior to baseball's December meetings in Chicago, however, Boston owner Taylor stopped off in Fort Wayne and convinced Stahl to serve as player-manager and team captain for 1907. On March 4, Stahl's Red Sox (the club's latest nickname) began spring training in Little Rock, Arkansas. One of the hardest workers in camp was Collins, who had returned to play third base for his old roommate. By month's end the Red Sox began wending their way north by train, playing exhibition games along the way in preparation for the April 11 season opener in Philadelphia.

At first glance Stahl's first season as big-league manager held promise. A headline in the March 23 edition of the *Sporting News* proclaimed: "Stahl Satisfied. Boston Team's Prospects are Bright." The manager, however, was a jumble of nerves. "You can't imagine how this job is affecting me," he confided during the team's stay in Little Rock. "I wish I had never taken it." Their manager, several Red Sox players whispered to reporters, seemed prone to "fits of melancholy and despondency." On Monday, March 25, in Louisville, Stahl abruptly resigned. The "manifold responsibilities" as manager, explained the *Sporting News*, had caused anxieties that affected Stahl's play on the field. Stahl did, however, retain his title as the team's captain.

Although relieved of the burden of command, Stahl still seemed depressed. Friends later recalled that while he was in Louisville Stahl had a "strange, wild look" and exhibited "great nervousness" even while he was on the field. During the train ride from Louisville to West Baden Springs, located about fifty miles to the northwest, Stahl talked with teammates about Win Mercer, a former Washington pitcher, and catcher Marty Bergen, one of Stahl's old National League teammates. Four years earlier Mercer had asphyxiated himself in a hotel room. In 1900 Bergen had taken an ax to his wife and children before shooting himself in a grisly murder-suicide.

Stahl's spirits seemed buoyed when he reached West Baden Springs. Boston's schedule included exhibition games in Indianapolis and Fort Wayne, where Stahl had legions of fans. On March 27 he sent a telegram to his wife Julia, who had left Fort Wayne for Roxbury after her husband had headed for spring training. "Cheer up little girl and be happy," the telegram read. "I am all right now and able to play the game of my life."

During their time in Indiana the Red Sox stayed at the West Baden Springs Hotel, where Stahl and Collins had adjoining rooms on the third floor. On March 28 Stahl rose early "in his usual good health and spirits," according to one account. He ate a hearty breakfast with several teammates and declared that it looked like a fine day for a ball game. At about 8:30 a.m. Stahl visited with the hotel's owner and spent fifteen minutes discussing bathhouse tickets for the Red Sox players. He and Collins headed up to their rooms and began to dress for practice. While Collins was still getting ready, Stahl walked in, stayed for a few minutes, and then went back to his own room. A few minutes later he returned and told his friend, "I don't feel right, Jimmy."

"What's the matter," Collins responded. "Where do you feel bad?"

Stahl, who appeared dazed, said he did not know and lay down on Collins's bed. As Stahl began to writhe in pain, Collins called for the hotel physician. Red Sox first baseman Bob Unglaub was passing by in the hallway and rushed into the room when he heard Collins call for help. Unglaub could smell carbolic acid, a germ-killing compound that, unless diluted, is a deadly poison. The acid had scalded Stahl's mouth and throat and was rapidly shutting down his lungs and blood flow.

"Why did you do this, old man?" Unglaub asked his teammate.

"Boys, I couldn't help it," Stahl managed to reply. "It drove me to it."

Within minutes Stahl was dead, a suicide victim at age thirty-four.

Stahl's teammates were stunned, particularly Collins. *Boston Post* reporter Fred O'Connell said that almost overnight Collins "looked ten years older and had black rings under his eyes." Stahl's family was overwhelmed with grief. Julia Stahl, widowed less than twenty weeks after her wedding day, swooned when she heard the news. "I should have been there before" was her only comment to the press as she boarded a train for Indiana the following day. The Stahls were Roman Catholics and, noted longtime baseball writer Fred Lieb, Chick "never forgot his religious duties." As a suicide, however, Stahl could not receive the funeral rites of the church. Services were conducted by the Fraternal Order of Eagles and the Benevolent Order of Elks—organizations to which Stahl belonged. On March 31, in the largest funeral Fort Wayne had ever seen, Stahl was buried in Lindenwood Cemetery.

Most newspaper accounts blamed Stahl's death on job pressures, but some stories began to surface indicating the ballplayer's carefree demeanor disguised morbid tendencies. Close friends told the *Fort Wayne Journal-Gazette* that when depressed, Stahl had talked about taking his own life as far back as his semipro days with the Pilseners. The *Fort Wayne Daily News* discussed the "tragedy of friendship" between Stahl and Collins, suggesting that Stahl had hoped to see Collins reinstated as Red Sox manager. When his attempts failed, intimated the newspaper, Stahl killed himself.

Others, however, believed that Stahl's motives were far less noble. They claimed it was a woman who drove the ballplayer to his drastic action. Stahl had always been very popular with female fans, including a Fort Wayne stenographer named Louisa "Lulu" Ortman. One night in January 1902, police arrested Ortman after she had accosted Stahl on a street in Fort Wayne and had aimed a revolver at him. Stahl had jilted her, Ortman told authorities, and she said she intended to kill him. Stahl declined to press charges against Ortman.

Baseball scholar Harold Seymour, in an exhaustive trilogy on the sport's history, wrote that Stahl may

Boston teammates pose with a group of children in Macon, Georgia, on Saint Patrick's Day in 1903. Jimmy Collins is the third player from the left, and Stahl stands to his right.

LEFT: Stahl prepares to towel off some sweat during the sixth game of the 1903 World Series pitting Boston against Pittsburgh. According to a Pittsburgh newspaper, Boston fans "acted . . . like escaped patients from an insane asylum" during the series. ABOVE: The Boston team in 1901. Top row, left to right: Fred Mitchell, Harry Kane, and Tommy Dowd. Middle row, left to right: Charlie Hemphill, Fred Parent, McKenna, Hobe Ferris, Win Kellum, Nig Cuppy, and Buck Freeman. Front row, left to right: Ossee Schreckengost, Lou Criger, Larry McLean, Jimmy Collins, Cy Young, and Chick Stahl.

A view of the stands at Exposition Park during a 1903 World Series game between Pittsburgh and Boston.

have been hounded by "a woman who asserted she was his pregnant wife." In the May 1986 edition of *Boston* magazine, Glenn Stout claimed that knowledge of the relationship between Stahl and this anonymous woman "survived as a whispered secret among baseball insiders." Stout buttressed his argument with veiled statements from contemporary reporters such as Tim Murnane of the *Boston Globe*, who indicated that "baseball affairs were only incidental" to Stahl's self-destruction, and the *Boston Post's* Fred O'Connell, who said in print that "many know the true cause" of the player's suicide. Stout maintained that Stahl had an affair with a woman in Chicago during the 1906 season and that during spring training a year later she began to blackmail him. "Her demands were simple," wrote Stout, "either Stahl would agree to marry her or she would tell the world about their expected child."

Pointing out that carbolic acid was used at the time as a treatment for venereal disease, Stout implied that Stahl had contracted syphilis. During an interview with Peter Golenbock for the book *Fenway: An Unexpurgated History of the Boston Red Sox*, Stout mentioned an unsubstantiated rumor that Stahl had infected Julia with the disease and that because of this she had left him and returned to Boston. A 1907 newspaper article, however, told about a party in Fort Wayne that the couple had attended about five weeks before Stahl's death. "Mr. Stahl was a happy man that night," according to the report, which quotes an eyewitness as saying that the Stahls "seemed entirely devoted to each other."

Another supposition holds that Stahl saw his playing career drawing to a close and decided to call it quits on his own terms. The *Fort Wayne Journal-Gazette* claimed that Stahl "feared the down-grade. He had a horror of having ever to appear before an audience in the role of one who has outlived his usefulness." Judging by Stahl's 1906 performance—he played 155 games, led American League outfielders with 344 putouts, batted .286, and homered in his final at bat of the season—he was far from over the hill.

Whether it was job pressures, trouble with women, fear of debilitation, or perhaps some combination, the reasons that drove Stahl to suicide have been buried with him for decades. Fate was kinder to Stahl's friend Collins, who retired after the 1908 season and was elected to the National Baseball Hall of Fame in 1945, two years after his death at age seventy-three. Taylor, the fractious Red Sox owner, sold the team in September 1911 after building it a new home, Fenway Park, which opened on April 20, 1912.

Julia Stahl died in Boston on November 16, 1908, twenty months after her husband's suicide. Even her demise added to speculation about the reasons for her husband's ruin. The cause of death was listed as "exhaustion brought on by the use of drugs and alcohol"—an overdose. Julia's own sad fate spurred gossip that it was her addiction that prompted Chick Stahl's last, desperate act.

John L. McQuown, 1942.

The Club with a Reputation

A History of the Dekalb County Boxing Club

Rachel S. Roberts

UNLESS OTHERWISE NOTED ALL ILLUSTRATIONS COURTESY JOHN McQUOWN AND RAY SAXER

Ray Mitchell liked to watch Burniston

box, liked to see Burniston get an open shot at his opponent's jaw. When "Burnie" got into the ring, anything could happen. Burniston could knock out his opponent's mouthpiece and land it anywhere from the first to the sixth row back. Once he knocked out three of his opponent's teeth. On this night, at the 1961 Muncie district Golden Gloves tournament, Ray Burniston was in top form, winning his first open championship in the 160-pound division and the chance to represent the DeKalb County Boxing Club in the Tournament of Champions in Chicago.

As a timekeeper for the club, Mitchell watched many young men excel in the sport of amateur boxing, including Arni "Sugar Toes" Placencia, Rival "Duge" McBride, and Jeff "Rocky" Rowe. Records show that in its thirty-seven-year history more than 1,800 members trained and boxed for the DeKalb County Boxing Club, amassing so many wins that it became the envy of other midwestern amateur boxing clubs.

Much of the credit for the club's success must go to its founders, Ray "Bud" Saxer and John L. McQuown, two Hoosiers who believed in giving boys a chance to learn the art of boxing and who coached and enjoyed the sport, not as spectators but as former participants. To appreciate or understand the history of the DeKalb County Boxing Club, it is helpful also to know about Saxer and McQuown's boyhood boxing experiences.

In 1937, at age seventeen, Saxer weighed only 124 pounds and was five feet, six inches tall. Ellsworth, his older brother, thought Bud should learn how to defend himself, and although he himself didn't know much about boxing, he made Bud a heavy bag, using a grain sack filled with rags and sawdust. The boys bought a speed bag and built a boxing ring in their dad's orchard. After reading everything they could find about boxing, they began sparring. Sometimes on weekends, Ellsworth would bring home some of his buddies to spar with his little brother, and in the fall of 1937 he began taking Bud to Fort Wayne to work out at the GE Club gym or the Wheatley Social Center.

By 1939 Bud figured he was ready for the Fort Wayne Golden Gloves tournament, but no one else thought so. His father was against the idea. Bud signed up anyway. It took only forty-seven seconds for the young boxer to realize his dad was right. Leaving the gym with a black eye, Bud heard the referee tell him to get more experience before coming back. Disappointed but determined, he decided to enter the 1940 Golden Gloves tournament. For that match, he would be ready. He would spar with anyone who dared. Soon he developed a reputation.

John McQuown of Auburn was small and wiry but born with a competitive spirit. As far back as he could remember, he challenged his friends and playmates in wrestling, sparring, and running matches. It was part of growing up on a farm where recreational facilities were limited. By the time he was in high school, he was winning more often than losing, and his friends decided to seek revenge. They devised a way to get back at him. They had heard about Bud Saxer of Garrett, who they believed would "knock the tar" out of him. They took McQuown to meet "the fellow with a reputation."

The match never took place. "We immediately liked each other and were eager to learn from the other," McQuown said. Since both were planning to enter the 1940 Fort Wayne Golden Gloves tournament, they decided to train together. Their sparring was good, the dynamics exciting. Their equipment was crude, but they made the best of it. They had a heavy punching bag, a jump rope, and some badly worn boxing gloves. The place where they met for sparring sessions had no heat, so they worked out in their street clothes.

By tournament time, both were in high spirits. McQuown competed in the featherweight division and Saxer in the lightweight division. Neither won titles, but it wasn't long before each was fighting his way into final-night action, sometimes gaining runner-up positions.

```
AUBURN ALUMNI GYMNASIUM
AUBURN, INDIANA
```

No. 1748

Wed.	**AMATEUR BOXING SHOW**
MAR.	Sanctioned by
	Indiana Ass'n Amateur Athletic Union of U.S.
20	Sponsored by
	Auburn Lions Club
1957	DeKalb County Boxing Club
	Management reserves the right to revoke this ticket by refunding money.
8:15 P.M.	General Admission 90c No Tax

The DeKalb County Boxing Club often held amateur shows in the Auburn Alumni Gymnasium. Sponsored by the Auburn Lions Club, they were a popular form of entertainment in the northeastern Indiana community.

World War II changed the young men's lives. McQuown entered an aircraft engineering school in Boston where he was soon recruited to initiate a boxing program. With every transfer, he continued boxing, even winning "Athlete of the Week" at the Sarasota air base after a loss to Elmo Escobar of Pinellas air base in what sportswriters of the day called "the closest decision of the season." Saxer, on the other hand, entered the army and was shipped to the South Pacific, where he fought not only the enemy but every boxer who would take him on. Later he recalled twenty-one fights in as many days. Those tournaments provided "a lot of entertainment for the personnel aboard ship," one account states, "as Saxer was on the winning side of most bouts."

When the two returned to Indiana, they became busy with their jobs and families. McQuown knew he could no longer compete with the new generation of boxers and decided he'd like to coach boxing. When Scoutmaster Leroy Close asked him to demonstrate the art of self-defense to Boy Scout Troop #169, he looked up Saxer.

McQuown and Saxer's demonstration was a success. Three of the nineteen Scouts who watched the program expressed interest in competing in a Golden Gloves tournament. McQuown and Saxer took the three, along with two other area boxers, and began training them.

The 1953 Golden Gloves tournament held in Fort Wayne was the beginning of an impressive record of successes for the DeKalb County Boxing Club. At that tournament, member Robert Walter won a championship and a chance to represent the Fort Wayne Golden Gloves team in Chicago. The DeKalb County boxers also had a runner-up, and two boys qualified for the semifinals. McQuown and Saxer were convinced that a local team could be a winning one.

With the help of a local attorney, Harold Stump, McQuown and Saxer drew up bylaws and rules and applied for membership in the Indiana Association of the Amateur Athletic Union, making the club official. "We adopted the name of our club from the late Karl Mavis, a local sportswriter who often referred to the group as 'the DeKalb County Boxing Club,'" McQuown wrote many years later in his memoirs. An empty lot on Saxer's farm in Garrett became known as "Saxer Field," and Saxer's garage, "the clubhouse." The GE Club of Fort Wayne lent some equipment to get the club started. All that was required for membership in the DeKalb County Boxing Club was that each boy pass a medical examination and present a permission slip signed by a parent or guardian. At first the qualifying age was set at sixteen, but when tournaments began adding novice and junior divisions, the club encouraged younger boys to participate. "We had boxers as young as nine," McQuown said, "and one who was thirty. The average age, however, was eleven up through high school." In the early days, junior boxers paid twenty-five cents to join the club—"just enough to cover the cost of having their membership cards printed," according to McQuown. Senior boxers paid a dollar. Later, when the AAU developed more stringent rules about insurance coverage, "we had to charge a little more—but never more than two dollars," McQuown said. Boxers did not have to live in DeKalb County to participate. As word about the club spread, many young men from surrounding communities asked to join and were welcomed.

ABOVE: Ray Saxer's friends gather in his backyard for boxing practice, 1939; FAR RIGHT: Garrett police officer Jerry Custer presents the Boxer of the Month award to Dave Walker in the mid-1970s; RIGHT: Robert Walter, winner of the DeKalb County Boxing Club's first Golden Gloves championship in 1953; BELOW: club officers in the late 1950s were (left to right) John McQuown, Robert Morr, Hobie Hart, and Ray Saxer.

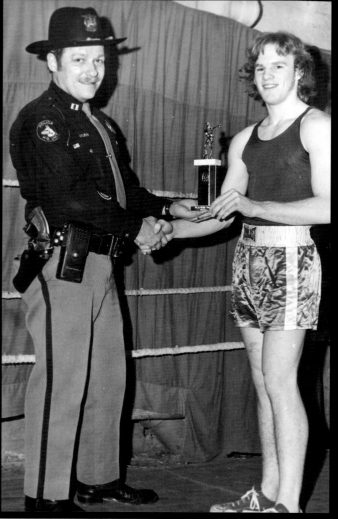

After months of planning, nineteen boxers went to Fort Wayne's Memorial Coliseum to represent the DeKalb County Boxing Club in the 1954 Golden Gloves tournament. The boys boxed in the novice division, the first time in the twenty-five-year history of the tournament that such a division was included, and fared well, winning three of the eight open divisions and two runner-up positions. The three champions joined an eight-man Fort Wayne team for the trip to Chicago for the Tournament of Champions.

three nights of competition it rated third among the twelve participants. By then the club had developed a "reputation." With uniforms, success, and enthusiasm, the DeKalb County Boxing Club set the standard for amateur boxing excellence in northeast Indiana.

In 1956 Hobie Hart was appointed boxing commissioner for the Indiana Association of the Amateur Athletic Union. Under his leadership, interest in amateur boxing continued to flourish. Hart believed it "only fair that a similarly high exact-

With uniforms, success, and enthusiasm, the DeKalb County Boxing Club set the standard for amateur boxing excellence in northeast Indiana.

Determined to find new outlets for their boxers, McQuown, Saxer, and two other officers, Robert Walter and Robert Baughman, spent hours not only training the young boys but also contacting clubs and organizations for equipment and support. Although membership fees were low, some of the boys didn't have the means to pay. "When that happened, either Saxer or I would give them an extra job sweeping or cleaning the clubhouse and then we'd take their fee from that," McQuown said. Businessman H. E. "Hobie" Hart of Auburn also helped. "He was a wonderful supporter, often slipping us a little money to help with expenses. I don't know what we would have done without him. God, he loved that club," recalled McQuown. The Auburn Lions Club also took note of the club's needs and donated sixteen pairs of boxing trunks in the club's green and white colors. On March 31, 1955, the Lions underwrote a boxing exhibition staged in the Auburn Alumni Gym. Approximately one thousand fans attended. The competition was tough because the DeKalb County boxers were matched with boxers representing Local 9 of the Toledo Glass Workers' Athletic Club. That night the audience enjoyed spectacular boxing.

In the 1956 Toledo Golden Gloves tournament, DeKalb was the only Indiana team entered, and after

ing standard should be imposed on those upon whom the responsibility is placed in deciding the winners," McQuown recorded in his notes. Consequently, a boxing clinic was held in Auburn for people interested in becoming judges, referees, timekeepers, or announcers, the first of several.

As the club became more active, leaders felt it would be helpful to have a portable elevated ring that could easily and quickly be assembled and disassembled. After talking it over, the club undertook the project. Hart, who owned the rides and concessions at the old Swinney Park in Fort Wayne, donated much of the lumber for the ring, most coming from dismantled buildings and rides at the park. The floor, donated by the Auburn Lions Club, was constructed of plywood and covered with foam padding. Someone found in his barn a stash of heavy rope that members used for the ring ropes. As a project, Boy Scout Troop #169 braided the ropes so that each would be identical without knots or bumps. The ropes were then wrapped with rags and old bedsheets.

It wasn't a fancy ring, but it served its purpose. The club used it for exhibitions and rented it as well, using the proceeds to cover the cost of other operating expenses. It was a welcome source of revenue. The project, which took hours of planning and fabrication,

Ray "Bud" Saxer, 1942. Auburn photographer Kelso Davis took this picture of Saxer and the picture of John McQuown on page fifty-four before Saxer and McQuown left DeKalb County to serve in World War II.

LEFT: **Dick Martin (left) fights Ronald Lee of Toledo in 1960.** RIGHT: **Ed Placencia (left) scores with a left hook, turning a 1976 state AAU tournament match in his favor. Placencia won the state tournament title for his weight class and represented Indiana at the national tournament held in Las Vegas.**

also taught the young members a great deal about business conduct and ethics.

Traditions soon developed. One was the "point system." Under this system, club leaders assigned points to boxers based on their conduct, sportsmanship, attendance, coachability, ability to get along with fellow members, and attitude toward the club. The boys could earn up to five points at any club session or function, at home or on the road. Officers kept records and at the end of the year announced winners and awarded trophies, many sponsored by area businesses. The first awards ceremony was held on January 12, 1955, and the recipients, selected from twenty-six active members, were brothers Rival and Jerald McBride of Garrett. Five years later, in 1960, the club awarded its first honor jackets. The jackets were high quality and in the club's colors of green, for the body, and white, for the sleeves and trim. On the back was the club's logo. In order to qualify for an honor jacket, a boxer had to accumulate a total of eight hundred points. Other popular awards were the "Fighter of the Night" designation, which began in 1956 and became a feature of nearly every boxing show, and the "Boxer of the Month" title, first awarded in 1971 to Matt Myers of Garrett.

One reward was particularly memorable for some

of the young members. On the last night of the boxing season in 1957, Hobie Hart stunned the club by announcing he would underwrite a wilderness trip to Canada for all eligible members. The point system would be used to determine eligibility. Eleven young members qualified. Because many of the boys had never traveled out of state, the Canadian fishing trip was the highlight of their lives. It was also an exciting trip for DeKalb residents as well because many organizations, residents, and families got involved in helping the boys prepare and plan. Hart purchased a used school bus from Saint Joe's Sechler pickle company, Auburn Motor Sales serviced it, and officers and members worked hours to construct a rack that would carry four aluminum boats and outboard motors. A grocer donated food; a doctor prepared and donated an elaborate emergency kit; and families assisted with provisions and tents.

While the community pulled together to support the club, members reciprocated. They presented matches to entertain the public and raise funds for local charities. Exhibits included the Fourth of July show at Garrett's Feick Park, the Kendallville matches in support of the Kendallville Youth Center, and several exhibitions in Garrett to raise funds for the Garrett baseball program. In 1957 the boxers held a show at the veterans hospital in Fort Wayne. The show was a hit and the topic of conversation for weeks. It became an annual tradition that lasted twenty-eight years.

Bud Saxer, called "the father of the club," was the "glue" that held the club together through the years. Recognizing his efforts and dedication, the city of Garrett named him Citizen of the Year in 1969, and the police honored him for giving many young men opportunities to get their lives "straightened out." Recognition of his efforts continued for many more years. On March 1, 1976, Police Chief Harold E. Werkheiser wrote, "Be it known that on this date, the Garrett Police Department recognized Mr. Ray 'Bud' Saxer for upstanding and meritorious service to the police department and the community as a whole. Mr. Saxer has given freely and unselfishly of his time to curb juvenile delinquency through his affiliation with the DeKalb Boxing Club."

Hundreds of young men agreed and credited the club for giving them a future. Wrote one, "I joined the boxing club for a number of reasons: most of them for the wrong reason . . . my ego. I wanted to be aggressive in a harmful way, to have people notice me, to be a big shot. I was always getting in trouble for fighting in the streets. . . . The club taught me to be able to handle situations that arose. It built personality and character." A testimonial in the form of a letter to the editor appeared in the newspaper: "Bud Saxer has kept many boys off the streets and out of trouble with the training he spends with the club, which is sometimes as high as four nights a week, training them so they are strong and alert and able to handle themselves well in the ring or on the gym floor." The letter was signed, "The parents and boys

As Russell Kruse announces, Ray Saxer (right) presents former world heavyweight champion Joe Louis with a DeKalb County Boxing Club cap at the 1976 state AAU tournament in Fort Wayne.

of the boxing club."

Newspaper clippings and records show that the DeKalb County Boxing Club produced winners. Twenty-two boxers either won as champions or runners-up in national Golden Gloves district and regional tournaments, with some advancing to national competitions. Ed Placencia of Garrett fought in the national AAU tournament in Las Vegas in 1976 and was elected captain of the Indiana team. Tom Esselburn participated in the Biloxi, Mississippi, national AAU tournament in 1978 and in many state Junior Olympic tournaments. In state AAU tournaments, Placencia, Esselburn, Dave Walker, Dan Somers, and Glen Boxell won matches and were named champions. Club statistics list many other DeKalb County Boxing Club members who became championship winners. In all, fifteen members of the DeKalb County Boxing Club fought in national Golden Gloves and AAU tournaments.

Saxer wrote that he thought the success of the organization was based on three tenets. First, everyone who signed up in the club got the same attention, went through the same training routine, and enjoyed the opportunity to participate in a sanctioned boxing show regardless of talent. All a boy had to do to qualify was to show his coaches he was in condition to box three strong rounds. Second, all coaches had previous boxing experience against good competition so they were able to prepare the members for any level of possible competition. Third, all members had the opportunity to participate in the making of the club rules. Whenever a problem arose in the club, the membership gathered, discussed the situation, and voted on how to solve the problem.

Coach Ray Saxer (right) helps members Max Wappes (left) and Rival McBride (center) prepare fish soup during the club's 1957 trip to Canada. Member Clayton Morr is in the background. "The fishing was fantastic," John McQuown wrote in his remembrances of the trip. "All were caught on Creek Chub lures, furnished by the famous Creek Chub Bait Company of Garrett, Indiana."

Arnold Placencia (top row, in jacket) travels with members of an Indiana delegation to the 1969 national Golden Gloves tournament in Kansas City, Missouri.

Along with Saxer and McQuown, other people helped make the club successful, and even the city of Garrett played a role. In 1972 the club held its first training session in its new quarters in the city hall basement, a move that answered the club's desperate need for additional training space. The Reverend James Waters of Garrett's First Baptist Church, who not only encouraged the group but gave money, was the one who first suggested the possibility of using the empty rooms in city hall. His idea worked. The move from Saxer's two-car garage gave the club more space for sparring and for equipment. Photographer Andy Wilbur was another friend. "Andy came any-time we called on him," recalled McQuown, "and he'd take pictures for the newspaper or to give to the boys." Russell Kruse and his son Dean were especially supportive, often giving the young boxers complimentary tickets to special boxing matches or arranging special events. Russell got former heavyweight champion Joe Louis involved. Louis handed out the

awards at the 1976 state AAU tournament in Fort Wayne, when the DeKalb County boxers showed their winning colors.

As the years passed, so did club leadership. Saxer and McQuown remained involved, but their roles changed. Ray Burniston, who once entertained Mitchell with his finesse, became the head coach in 1971, and Saxer served as his manager. When Burniston moved, former member Ed Placencia accepted the position, serving as head coach for thirteen years. "As much as I enjoyed the boxing, nothing ever meant more to me than the coaching I was fortunate enough to administer," Placencia wrote in 1992. At different times, Ed Placencia was assisted by former club boxers Ruben Gonzalez, Dave Placencia, and Randy Brown. It was gratifying to the founders that when members were unable to participate in the ring, they remained committed as volunteers, coaches, or officers. The success of the DeKalb County Boxing Club had much to do

TOP: **Champions and runners-up at the 1954 Fort Wayne Golden Gloves tournament. Front row (left to right): John McBride, Jerald McBride, and Lawrence Weidler. Middle row (left to right): Coach Robert Walter, Jimmy Reeder, Oscar Ayers, and Coach John McQuown. Back row (left to right): Coaches Ray Saxer and Robert Baughman.** BOTTOM: **The recipients of the first honor jackets, awarded in 1960, were (left to right) Jerald McBride, John Placencia, John McBride, Ray Burniston, Rival McBride, Dick Martin, and Howard Shaw.**

with the consistency of leadership, which was strong, honest, and professional. None of the coaches received remuneration for his efforts.

Despite this dedication, in 1989 an official announcement appeared in the local newspapers stating that the club was disbanding. There were two main reasons. One was that the city of Garrett needed its rooms in the basement of city hall. The club's officers held an intensive search for alternate training space, but none was found that was suitable. The other reason for disbanding was that the focus of the club had changed. McQuown explained that increasingly young men weren't joining the club to train for boxing competitions but were looking for a place to "hang out" or simply to exercise, and because the YMCA had programs in place that could provide those opportunities, the DeKalb County Boxing Club coaches, recognizing their interest was to coach boxing, felt it was time to hang up their gloves.

Among the many accomplishments of the club, several deserve mention. As early as the 1950s when the racial timbre of American culture was more delicate, the DeKalb County Boxing Club showed no prejudices. When Dick Martin, a black seventeen-year-old from Alabama, moved to Fort Wayne, he made inquiries and was immediately accepted. He recalls, "Times were tough back then and I often found myself short on funds for gasoline to make the trip to Garrett for training sessions, but I always seemed to get there somehow." He also tells of a time when he was in the ring and showed some hesitancy. "Bud told me I should have been a preacher instead of a boxer. I will never forget that. Well, I never became a preacher, but I am very active [in church]." He credits the DeKalb County Boxing Club with giving him the tools to deal with life.

Women were also active in the club. In 1973 Claudia Morr qualified as a judge and was recognized as "know[ing] the AAU boxing rule book forward and backwards." The fact that husband James and son Pat were involved in the club contributed to her interest, but "anytime her son happened to be in the ring," said McQuown, "she had the good sense to excuse herself from the judging." Evie Esselburn, a typical volunteer, and others pitched in to keep uniforms clean and mended, to help with banquets, or to drive boxers to tournaments.

The club can be proud of its positive influence on building relationships; it connected families and extended across generations. Entire families got involved, including the Placencia brothers—John, Ed, Dave, Gene, Arni, Rick, and Ray—each making a name for himself as an outstanding boxer. Several Placencias also contributed as coaches. Four Boxell brothers went through the club's programs, as did four McBrides, four Warricks, and three generations of the Morr family. The membership lists the Fraze brothers, the Esselburns, the Mettert boys, and others.

The boys who went through the DeKalb County Boxing Club are now grown or have died. Those who sent letters to be included in a collection of memories tell about their present lives and occupations. Some graduated from universities with high honors; others went into the military. One became a minister and is a chaplain, a lieutenant commander. Another works for NASA. Several went into construction, and many went into business for themselves. Many who were given that "one last chance" credit the club with turning their lives around.

A letter sent to former members states, "Throughout the years we have watched many frail young boys grow and develop into husky, muscular, confident young men. We have reluctantly watched members go off to war, many becoming highly decorated heroes. We have mourned for those who gave the supreme sacrifice. We have been pleased to see former members become respected citizens, community leaders, and successful businessmen. . . . If any of the lessons learned in the boxing club has contributed in a positive manner in the transformation from youth to manhood, we have been richly rewarded." The letter was signed, "All former DeKalb County Boxing Club Officers, Coaches, and Trainers."

Nearly two thousand names are on the club's old rosters. Looking over the list McQuown said simply, "Each one was a fine young man."

Bob Jewell, winner of the Indiana High School Athletic Association's 1951 Trester Award for mental attitude. After graduating from Attucks, Jewell played basketball at the University of Michigan and Indiana Central College, then began a successful career as a clinical researcher with Indianapolis's Eli Lilly and Company.

The Shot

Crispus Attucks Tigers vs. Anderson Indians
Randy Roberts

There were no doubts now; they would win this 1951 regional title game, take advantage of a weak semistate division, then capture their fourth state championship. Not that Attucks, with a record of 23 and 1, hadn't provided a few tense moments. Midway through the second quarter the Crispus Attucks Tigers, the all-black team from the west side of Indianapolis, had led the Anderson Indians 45–30, but that lead had narrowed to 45–37 at the half. Then in the second half, Anderson had slowed down Attucks's fast-break game, hit their own shots, taken advantage of several "suspicious" calls by the referees, and moved into the lead. Anderson led by five at the end of the third quarter, and ten with only four and a half minutes left in the game. Even the Attucks supporters, the sea of black faces stuffed into a corner of Indianapolis's Butler Fieldhouse, seemed to have accepted the inevitable. "There was simply no way those black kids were going to win," remembered an Anderson fan.

To make matters worse, John "Noon" Davis, Crispus Attucks's fine forward, had just been called for his fifth foul. His head bent and shoulders rounded, he slouched to the bench, hardly exchanging a word with his substitute, five foot, nine inch sophomore Bailey "Flap" Robertson. In the stands a smattering of polite applause mixed with shouts of encouragement from the Attucks section.

Nobody was really sure how Bailey got pegged with the name "Flap." Some said it was the direct result of his loose-wristed shooting and running style. There was an exaggerated pronation and forward extension about his shot. "It was like he was waving at the ball as it left for the hoop," recalled his friend Bill Scott. "And when he ran his hand just kept flappin'." Bill Swatts, another friend from Flap's high school days, was not so sure about the shooting theory. He recalled hearing that Bailey had gotten the name as a result of the old sneakers he used to wear. "We were poor kids. Our parents couldn't afford new shoes. We'd wear them off our feet. Sometimes the lower rubber section would split from the upper canvas part. We'd just wrap them with tape." But the quick playground fix never lasted long, and soon the upper and lower would gape like an open mouth and start flapping as the player ran. Anyway, that's how Swatts believed Bailey got his name. But he admits that there is still another theory that might be true. "Bailey was a talker. Talked all the time. 'Always flappin' his mouth,' some said." Shooting, running, talking—doesn't make any difference. The name fit and stuck.

If Flap Robertson was nervous about playing in the most important game in the history of Crispus Attucks, he did not show it. Through some error, his name had been left off the roster during the sectional tournament. As he later recalled, "When I got a chance to play in the regional, I wanted to make sure the coach would remember who I was." No sooner did he touch the ball than he shot it, a fifteen-foot jumper that cut the spread to eight points and, according to Jim Cummings, a writer for the African American *Indianapolis Recorder*, "rekindled a spark of hope in Attucks hearts." His prose might have been a little heated and partisan, but Cummings was nonetheless accurate. "If sophomore Bailey Robertson—who didn't even play in the sectional games—could score so easily, so can we," seemed the sentiment of the older players.

Willie Gardner—taller, thinner, poorer than most of the other kids on the team—made two quick baskets. The six foot, eight inch Gardner had joined the team at midseason, and since then Attucks had not lost a game. And if he could help it, they would not lose this one. Bob Jewell, the Attucks player whom every parent held up as an example of how to behave, helped Gardner by making a free throw. In one minute and twenty-nine seconds the Anderson lead had shrunk to three points, 72–69. "I've never heard anything like it," commented a person who was at the game. It was almost as if the fifteen thousand people watching the game had been divided along racial lines as they entered the barnlike Butler Fieldhouse, whites going to the choice seats and blacks relegated to the area behind the Attucks bench and in the back bleachers, where all the police congregated. But as Crispus Attucks struggled to get back in the game, the black corner was alive with activity. Some people were crying, a few had fainted. Anderson fans were also screaming, but a frantic note had replaced the smugness.

Sitting close to the floor, Crispus Attucks's principal Russell Lane and athletic director Alonzo Watford were as nervous as the other Tiger supporters. But they were less concerned about the game than the behavior

Willie Gardner (left) and Hallie Bryant (right) with their high school basketball coach, Ray Crowe. After high school, Gardner played for the Harlem Globetrotters and the New York Knickerbockers. Bryant played for Branch McCracken at Indiana University, leading the 1957 Hoosiers to a Big Ten championship, then joined the Globetrotters.

of the team and fans. On the court the players raced about frantically, their desire and their passion palpable. In the Attucks stands spectators screamed their encouragement, loud, holding nothing back. Across the floor Anderson fans cheered just as zealously, adding a racial edge to their cries of support. "Shamefully partisan," *Indianapolis Star* sportswriter Bob Collins would later describe the behavior of the Anderson fans. In this atmosphere anything could—might—happen. A wild scramble for the ball. A heatedly contested call. A fight on the court. A brawl in the stands. Anything. Lane and Watford had labored to get their school included in the state tournament, giving their black players a chance to compete against the white players. They had not—definitely not—sought an emotional confrontation. They had not wanted this.

But the game had leaped beyond them. Anderson pushed the ball up the court fast and out of control and turned it over. Gardner got the ball once again.

He drove toward the basket, began to shoot, and was hacked. Clearly, as far as Attucks supporters were concerned, a two-shot foul. But the referee signaled that Gardner was not shooting. One shot. His free throw cut the Anderson lead to 72–70. No sooner had Anderson's J. D. Alder increased his team's margin to 74–70 than Attucks's Hallie Bryant reduced it to two again with a twisting turnaround shot. The Crispus Attucks corner exploded with noise, breaking into the "Crazy Song." They sang,

Oh, Anderson is rough
And Anderson is tough
They can beat everybody
But they can't beat us
Hi-de-hi-de, hi-de-hi
Hi-de-hi-de, hi-de-ho
That's the skip, bob, beat-um
That's the crazy song.

The 1950–51 Anderson Indians finished their season with a record of 16–9. Front row: Manager Al Jackson, Don Dixon, Kent Poore, and Manager Jerry Phillips. Middle row: John Clemons, Frank Rousey, Herb Hood, Haynes Harrington, Bob McClain, and Chuck Smith. Back row: Assistant Coach James Early, Jerry Banker, Don Granger, J. D. Alder, Jack Tilley, and Head Coach Keith Lambert.

A referee's whistle cut into the celebration. A touch foul. Willie Gardner's fifth. He was out. Gardner, a future Harlem Globetrotter, joined fellow starter John Davis on the bench. Anderson increased its lead to 75–72. Two minutes and thirty-eight seconds remained in the game.

But Attucks kept fighting, and they had the players to do it. As a result of the segregationist educational policies in Indianapolis, the school did not have to depend on one good player, or two, or three. The team was loaded. With Gardner out of the game, sophomore Hallie Bryant, another future Globetrotter, took over. He grabbed an inbounds pass, drove the length of the court, and scored. Then he helped force a turnover and made another twisting shot from the top of the key, giving Attucks a 76–75 lead. Bob Collins called Bryant's performance under extraordinary pressure "above words," and he characterized the entire game as a time when "the unusual became commonplace, the improbable easy."

Gradually during the second half of the game the referees had been exerting more control. With alarming regularity they awarded two shots to Anderson for Attucks's fouls and one to Attucks for Anderson's fouls. Crispus Attucks head coach Ray Crowe and assistant coach Al Spurlock believed that their players were capable of winning the game, but they were not sure the officials would allow them. "I was kind'a scared because of the bad officiating," Spurlock admitted after the game. "By the end of the game it seemed as if Anderson had seven players on the court—two with striped uniforms," he added years later.

For a time the game became a free-throw contest. Anderson's high scorer, J. D. Alder, made two, giving his team a one-point lead. Attucks's Benny Cook missed two, but Jewell tipped in the second, taking the lead back. Next time up the court Cook was fouled again, making one of two this time. Crispus Attucks now led 79–77.

Benny Cook then turned from hackee to hacker. In quick succession he fouled Herb Hood and Jack Tilley. Hood made one of his two free throws; Tilley, pale and tired, made both of his. With twenty-three seconds remaining in the game, Anderson led 80–79.

In his mother's home on Colton Street, thirteen-year-old Oscar Robertson watched the game, proud of the black athletes running up and down the court. He had heard of other great black athletes, mostly boxers like Joe Louis, Sugar Ray Robinson, and Kid Gavilan. He had even listened to their fights on the radio. But now the faces on television were familiar; one was Flap's, his brother's. Though this was the first Crispus Attucks game Oscar had ever seen, he immediately grasped its importance. This was "something"—something in a city, a land, that offered

Ray Crowe first served as head coach at Crispus Attucks during the 1950–51 season. Members of that season's team were (clockwise from lower left): Charles Cook, Pervis Henderson, Benny Cook, Dejuain Boyd, Hallie Bryant, John "Noon" Davis, Charles West, Larry O'Banion, Charles "T" Toliver, William Mitchell, Bailey Robertson, and Stanley Warren. Not pictured are Leahman Covington, Willie Gardner, and Bob Jewell.

On the court, ten sets of players' eyes watched the ball. Two sets of officials' eyes watched the ball. Coaches, players on the bench, spectators in the stands, television viewers—they all watched the same ball.

nothing to blacks. Except for school, there was little to which Oscar looked forward. Gangs, white and black, had kept him pinned in his west-side neighborhood; poverty and racism had barred him from most entertainment facilities. In a way that he did not fully understand at the time, the game on the television screen gave him hope.

Twenty-three seconds. Benny Cook and Flap Robertson brought the ball up the court against light defense. In front of the Attucks bench, coaches Crowe and Spurlock tried to get their players' and the referees' attention. They wanted a time-out, a chance to set up a play. Nobody, not the players, officials, or spectators, paid them the slightest attention. With twelve seconds left the ball was in the hands of Charlie West, a substitute forward who had made only one basket during the game but knew what it took to become a high school legend. He drove hard for the basket, pulled up, and attempted an acrobatic scoop shot. The ball fell short and set off a mad scramble that ended when Jack Tilley kicked it out of bounds. Attucks ball. Seven seconds.

Sitting high in the bleachers, Bailey Robertson Sr. observed the game with interest but without wild passion. In the din swirling around him, he was the quiet center. When a friend asked him why, all he said was, "There's ten boys out on that court. Five are going to win and five are going to lose." Sure he felt proud that his son was part of the action, but something in him already identified with the five who would lose.

Bob Jewell held up two fingers to set up an out-of-bounds play. He lifted the ball over his head. He did not intend to throw it to Flap Robertson, but Hallie Bryant was covered and Robertson was not. Flap caught the ball on the baseline far in the corner. Not looking for Bryant or anyone else, he jumped, cocked his wrist in his unusual style, and released it. "I just grabbed the ball, shot and prayed," he later told a reporter. Different people remembered the shot differently. Many recalled that it was a flat, archless shot that struck the side of the rim and bounded straight

up. The ball kept climbing up and up, eight feet or more some would later say. Others, perhaps less inclined to poetic exaggeration, offered the opinion that the ball bounced only two or three feet above the rim. Coach Ray Crowe, however, insisted that the shot floated toward the basket with a lovely, high, glorious arch. In any case, it hung in the air above the rim long enough to seem like forever, a pregnant pause that delayed victory or defeat.

On the court, ten sets of players' eyes watched the ball. Two sets of officials' eyes watched the ball. Coaches, players on the bench, spectators in the stands, television viewers—they all watched the same ball. Oscar Robertson, sitting with his mother, Mazell, watched.

It fell straight through the hoop. Crispus Attucks won 81–80 in what a deeply proud *Indianapolis Recorder* reporter called "without a doubt, one of the most thrilling high school basketball games ever played in Indiana—or the world." Bob Collins, sportswriter for the *Indianapolis Star*, was considerably less partisan but no less impressed, labeling the game "the most dramatic and exciting" in tournament history. Flap Robertson recalled, "Later people told me their relatives died of heart attacks. One lady said she started to go into labor when the ball went through."

The black crowd erupted in a spontaneous celebration. But that outburst could not match the mood in west Indianapolis. As soon as the game ended the streets in the black section of the city bustled with activity. The heart of the street celebrations was Indiana Avenue, once the glittering center of Indianapolis African American nightlife. Indiana Avenue was still the hub, but much of the glitter was gone. But on this night no one noticed the decline. Traffic crawled up and down the avenue, emitting horn blasts and cries of joy. "Ba-ad, ba-a-ad Tigers," smiling residents greeted one another, then talked about the game and the certainty of upcoming semifinal and state victories.

White Indianapolis authorities were not sure what to make of either the victory or the celebrations. Crispus Attucks was, after all, a local team, and few

IHS, *Indianapolis Recorder Collection*, C7248

Alonzo Watford, Crispus Attucks High School's athletic director, in 1955. Watford, a star football player at Lafayette Jefferson High School and Butler University, also coached the Attucks football team and ended his career with a cumulative record of 150–33–3.

local teams had ever seemed as talented as the Tigers. But it was a local team without a white player, and the excitement along Indiana Avenue was vaguely disquieting, almost as if the servants had taken over the house for a party. Just to be on the safe side, Audry Jacobs, head of the police traffic division, sent extra patrolmen to the west side and toured the area himself.

An hour or so after the game ended Coach Crowe and his team arrived to take part in the festivities. They ate a late dinner of ham and sweet potatoes at Seldon's Cafe, stopping often to shake a hand or acknowledge a greeting. They were tired and very happy, and newspapers reported that after dinner they walked to Crispus Attucks for a bonfire and a snake dance. It was early in the morning by the time they began to float toward home.

Long before Flap arrived home, Oscar Robertson was in bed and asleep. But somehow his life would never be the same. His world, and the world of his black Indianapolis neighbors, had somehow, almost magically, expanded. Something different had happened, something that produced joy and hope. It

was almost as if Joe Louis was a local fighter and had knocked out Max Schmeling in Indianapolis. And his brother Flap had played a key role in the event. The name—Robertson—had taken on new meaning for every person he knew. Basketball and joy, race and achievement, had begun to come together.

The game had odd powers. Like great art, it had the ability to transcend and transform reality. It could raise players and spectators above their sometimes squalid and mundane lives or torpedo them into abject depression, and in that sense it was always more than a game. It was the intersection of art and politics, community and finance—and this was evident in no year more than 1951. While the drama of the Crispus Attucks Tigers occupied center stage in Indiana, another, far darker performance was running its course in New York City. Like ill-matched teammates, beside the Crispus Attucks stories in the Indianapolis newspapers lurked the unfolding drama of the 1951 basketball scandals.

At the beginning of 1951 college basketball was king. The National Invitational Tournament (NIT) attracted interest throughout the country, the National Collegiate Athletic Association (NCAA) tournament was growing in popularity, and conference races occupied the attention of millions of basketball fans during the long winter months. But with so much attention and such fanatical supporters, the sport also gained a devoted following among organized and unorganized crime. The point spread seemed tailored for basketball and its players. In theory—and often enough in reality—a few talented players on a good team could control, or at least influence, the margin of victory. They could play well enough for their team to win but not well enough to beat the point spread. It was a win-win proposition—win the game, win the bets. And by 1951 every wise guy on the streets knew that many of the best players in the country were active in both pursuits.

In early 1951 what was bound to happen did. The crime of "point shaving" and game fixing found its

Russell Lane taught English at Crispus Attucks when the school opened in 1927. In 1930 he became principal and served twenty-seven years before leaving in 1957 to accept an administrative position with Indianapolis Public Schools.

College, although Hogan, a good Catholic, steered his investigation away from the latter school. But Hogan also uncovered fixers at such leading midwestern universities as Toledo, Bradley, and Kentucky.

Midwestern fish were the last Hogan trolled. While Crispus Attucks was competing in the Indiana high school championship tournament, it was still possible for midwesterners to believe that the fixes were a northeastern, urban problem, mainly confined to blacks, Jews, Italians, and other "shady types." "Out here in the Midwest these scandalous conditions, of course, do not exist," the sanctimonious University of Kansas coach Forrest "Phog" Allen told reporters. "But in the East, the boys, particularly those who participate in the resort hotel leagues during the summer months, are thrown into an environment which cannot help but breed the evil which more and more is coming to light." The equally self-righteous University of Kentucky coach Adolph Rupp agreed: "Gamblers couldn't touch my boys with a ten-foot pole." In short, midwesterners observed a clear difference between the ethnically diverse urban players and the wholesome, generally WASPish heartland athletes.

Black and urban, Crispus Attucks found itself outside the cozy parameters of midwestern sports. But its victory over Anderson brought it inside the tent, much to the discomfort of many Hoosiers. Although every now and then the name Indianapolis Crispus Attucks—a modifier never before attached to the school—appeared in a newspaper, most editors gave more space to Attucks's seemingly over-energetic victory celebrations. Cries of "Ba-ad, ba-a-ad Tigers," long-lined snake dances, and meals of greens and sweet potato pie clued white Hoosiers everywhere

way to the desk of Manhattan district attorney Frank Hogan, a midlevel public servant with high-level ambitions. It was not the hardest criminal nut to crack; most of the players who had accepted bribes were decent enough college kids who began blabbing and blubbering as soon as they reached the inside of a police station, and often even before. So many players were involved that Hogan's main difficulty was choosing where to begin. For example, the City College of New York, the 1950 NIT and NCAA champions, was rich in fixers. At one time or another during the season all five starters and the top two reserves had shaved points or fixed games. At times different players blew shots, flubbed rebounds, and tossed errant passes for different gambling syndicates, occasionally at cross-purposes. Only the spread of the scandal deflected some of the public attention away from CCNY. New York schools absorbed the most punishing blows. Serious problems surfaced at Long Island University, New York University, Manhattan College, and Saint John's

COURTESY RAY CROWE

The 1950–51 Crispus Attucks basketball team celebrates a postseason win.

that Crispus Attucks was a world apart from Anderson.

But the school had a spot in the semifinals the following Saturday, and Anderson did not. Not since 1945 had an Indianapolis team made it to the state finals. With two victories at the semifinal tournament in Butler Fieldhouse Crispus Attucks could end that unseemly embarrassment. The Tigers accomplished both with remarkable ease. In the afternoon game they played Covington, whose coach promised that his team would control "the two big boys" (Bob Jewell and Willie Gardner) and contain the Crispus Attucks fast break. Once the game began, Covington players promptly ignored their coach and lost by forty points, the biggest spread since

1916. The evening contest was not much tighter. Attucks swept past Batesville 62-42, making it only the fourth city school to reach the final four.

Once again black residents of Indianapolis celebrated. Along Indiana Avenue Attucks faithful expressed their certainty that their team would capture the state title the following week: "It's in the bag." "The cup is ours." Once again the team ate a late dinner at Seldon's Cafe, and a victory bonfire burned early into the morning. But school officials celebrated in a subdued manner, voicing pride but nothing even approaching overconfidence. Alonzo Watford spoke of the quality of their next opponent and the need for continued sportsmanship, not the

Crispus Attucks basketball legends Bailey Robertson, Oscar Robertson, and Willie Gardner join Alonzo Watford (left), Attucks athletic director, and Bennie Charleston (right), an Indianapolis resident who helped promote local athletes, in a ribbon-cutting ceremony.

margin of their recent victories.

During the next week talk of race and basketball mixed uneasily in the newspapers, streets, and offices of Indianapolis, creating official and unofficial sub-texts. The official line was that race did not matter. *The Indianapolis Recorder* was so insistent on this point that any reader might conclude if, in fact, race was unimportant why did it need to be mentioned so often. In one article, a *Recorder* writer observed that Attucks would play in the state tournament "not alone for their school . . . but for the honor of their city and the pride of their fellow townsmen." White and black Indianapolis residents, he claimed, supported Crispus Attucks. An ugly incident in the Attucks-Batesville game demonstrated the city's solidarity. Early in the contest, a white drunk bellowed out, "Stop the niggers! I'm for the whites—I'm always for the whites!" And when several young white girls sitting close to him began cheering for Crispus Attucks, he told them, "Now you girls can all go down on the Avenue and get raped." At that point a white man turned around, angrily saying, "Listen, mister. I am from Indianapolis, and that team out there is our

Indianapolis team! That color talk of yours doesn't enter into it." Another white man added, "And that goes for me, too."

But submerged even in these denials that race mattered was the message that sport was the reason for the unexpected harmony. "Many a white has put the Satan of race prejudice behind him and jumped wholeheartedly on the Attucks bandwagon," observed an editorialist. "All this is eminently to the good. Our city has needed something like this, to erase the hostility built up by race-mongering. . . . It is cheering to discover that old Naptown has a heart after all, and that the spark of humanity still resides in the breast of the average Hoosier. Where the appeals of religion, reason and education seem to have fallen on deaf ears, the spectacle of brilliant basketball has turned the trick. In deep humility we observe that God does move in mysterious ways."

Not everyone, of course, followed the official line. Many Attucks supporters argued that race was important and that it did matter. They pointed to the close calls that always seemed to go against their school. Race mattered to the referees. They decried the health of a city where Hallie Bryant, Willie Gardner, and John Davis were cheered on the basketball court but could not find decent summer jobs, move freely about their city, or eat in restaurants where their exploits provided dinner conversation. In all significant ways, race still mattered.

Willie Gardner recalled the mood of the times: "We were a group of fifteen and sixteen-year-old kids who were just as tickled about winning as any group would have been and I'm sure that was the same case for our fans. But the larger community thought we were animals or something. I have no idea what would make them think that way. We were taught from day one that if we ever did anything stupid, then the whole school and community would suffer. That stuff didn't bother us. We'd come to expect it. But, as I got older, I wondered what ever made those people think we were interested in destroying our own community and school."

The reality of life in Indianapolis gave rise to the unofficial line: race relations would be damaged if Crispus Attucks won the state crown. This was the subtlest of messages, undocumented by newspaper articles or official memorandums. It was simply a feeling, passed down from the city fathers to principal Russell Lane to Coach Crowe and his players. There was no talk of intentionally losing—this was not a point-shaving scandal—just instructions to not press so hard and to be good sportsmen above all else. Throughout the tournament Lane had attended practices, addressing players as a team and talking to them in private, reminding them to play hard but play clean.

Shortly before Crispus Attucks's afternoon game with Evansville Reitz in the state tournament, Lane once again spoke with Crowe's team. Cheering pierced the walls of the locker room. The players were preparing for the game, thinking only about winning. Lane gave them something else to consider. Short and simple: "You are representing much more than your school. . . . You are black Indianapolis. This time, the whole state is watching. More important than winning is that you demonstrate good sportsmanship. Be gentlemen." Willie Gardner tuned Lane out. Bob Jewell, a product of a middle-class family from the more affluent north side—a student council president who had played Dr. Lane on Student Day—listened. He had never fouled out of a game. He was a gentleman. He would play like one.

The game began like a hundred-yard dash. Conventional wisdom held that the only way to defeat Crispus Attucks was to play a slow, controlled game. Reitz did the opposite. They ran and shot, repeatedly taking advantage of Attucks's soft defense. They also were more concerned with winning than sportsmanship, and according to one reporter "used a little more muscle and were a little less clean than the Tigers." Reitz's center, Jerry Whitesell, dined on Jewell's generous gentlemanly defense, leading his team with nineteen points. Adding to Attucks's problems, consistently throughout the game close calls

and "questionable calls" went in Reitz's favor. Whenever Attucks took or threatened to take the lead its players were whistled for fouls. For instance, toward the end of the third quarter, with Attucks leading 46–45, a Reitz player grabbed a rebound under the Tigers' basket but came down out-of-bounds. As the clock continued to tick, the referees conferred, finally handing the ball to Reitz. Although Attucks crept within one point of Reitz late in the fourth quarter—when another call went against the Tigers—the Evansville school won the game 66–59.

In defeat Attucks supporters sought consolation. If their team had not played particularly well, it had played cleanly. Jewell might have been outplayed, but he had not been "out-gentlemanned." He won the coveted Arthur L. Trester Award—named after a man who had struggled long and hard to keep black teams out of the state championships—for the player who best exemplifies "the ideal of the scholar-athlete-citizen." Years later Jewell still remembered the empty feeling. Being a gentleman was still important, but losing in the state finals hurt bad. "It was a Band-aid on a gaping wound," he said of the Trester Award.

If the Crispus Attucks run in 1951 had not ended with a state title, it had raised the possibility, so long submerged in the Indianapolis black community, of success—complete, uplifting, seldom-even-considered, beautiful success. Victory. Someday.

After the run Oscar Robertson became consumed by the game. That Christmas he got an orange ball. He dribbled it to school. He played on the local courts after classes, and at the Y when the wind and snow drove the players inside. He asked Willie Gardner and Hallie Bryant and his brother Flap how they did certain things. They talked, he listened. They taught, he learned. And he practiced and played, played and practiced.

A Major League Friendship

Carl Erskine Remembers Jackie Robinson and the Brooklyn Dodgers

Robert Gildea

The opening of the major league baseball season in April 1947 will long be remembered as an important line of demarcation in both the annals of the sport and American social history.

When Jack Roosevelt (Jackie) Robinson, a black infielder, took the field for the Brooklyn Dodgers that spring, a seventy-one-year pattern of racial segregation came to an abrupt but grudging end. By breaking the color barrier in a professional sport that previously had been all white, Jackie Robinson instantly became an American folk hero to millions of African Americans—and a significant symbol of the slowly evolving civil rights movement.

Over the next decade, Robinson established himself as one of baseball's most versatile and talented performers of all time. A .311 lifetime bat-

insights about another ballplayer with Indiana connections: Petersburg's Gil Hodges.

RLG: Carl, you weren't with the Dodgers in 1947 when Jackie Robinson broke in. Where were you in 1947, and under what circumstances did you first meet Jackie Robinson?

Erskine: Yes, you're right. Jackie and I were both signed by Branch Rickey prior to 1947. I signed in 1946, and Jackie signed in late 1945 and started in 1946. So, we were coming along together but not in the same place. I started in Danville, Illinois, in the Three-I League. I had just gotten out of the navy at age nineteen and signed a Class B contract. Jackie was in Montreal in 1946. In 1947 I had to go back to the same league because I'd had only a couple of months there, while Jackie moved

During his decade in the major leagues, Robinson befriended Dodger pitcher Carl Erskine, a young right-hander from Anderson, Indiana, who posted 122 victories for the team from Flatbush in a twelve-year career.

ting average, consistent infield play, daring exploits on the base paths, and a fiery disposition that spurred his teammates earned Robinson a spot in baseball's Hall of Fame in 1962—five years after his retirement and in his first year of voting eligibility.

During his decade in the major leagues, Robinson befriended Dodger pitcher Carl Erskine, a young right-hander from Anderson, Indiana, who posted 122 victories for the team from Flatbush in a twelve-year career. Robinson and Erskine became close comrades both on and off the field, and the laid-back Hoosier was confidant and counselor in helping Robinson resist retaliation against continuing displays of bigotry.

In the following interview with Robert L. Gildea, Erskine shares his recollections of Jackie Robinson—a portrait that expresses deep admiration for both the athlete and the man and simultaneously acknowledges his foibles. He also offers

on up to the Dodgers in 1947 and played in his first major league season. Of course, that was historic, and I missed that season.

But the next spring I was with Fort Worth, a Double A team, and the Dodgers came through Fort Worth to play an exhibition game. I didn't know anybody on the big team—on the "big club" as we called it—but I was pitching that day in this exhibition game prior to the start of the season. Each of our pitchers pitched three or four innings. I pitched the first three or four innings. The Dodgers won, of course, although they didn't score off me. When the game was over, I'm over on the bench on the visitors' side. Across the field comes this black ballplayer named Jackie Robinson. I had never met him, and to my surprise he says, "Where's Erskine?" I was shocked that he knew my name. So I walked up to him and spoke to him. He said, "Son, I just wanted to tell you, I hit against

Among Erskine's teammates were (left to right) Duke Snider, Jackie Robinson, Roy Campanella, Pee Wee Reese, and Gil Hodges. All but Hodges are Hall of Famers.

you today, and with the stuff you're throwing you're not going to be in this league very long." And that's how I met Jackie.

Two months later, after I had won about fifteen games in two-and-a-half months, the Dodgers called me up. I joined them in Pittsburgh. It was a Sunday afternoon. I walked into the clubhouse, didn't know a soul, was scared to death, had my duffel bag, and was looking for a locker and over came Jackie Robinson. He stuck out his hand with a big smile and said, "I told you, you wouldn't be down there very long." These were our initial meetings, and Jackie and I became very close friends. Even in our post-playing days, we continued to write each other and occasionally did some functions together.

RLG: There are a lot of stories about Jackie Robinson experiencing racial discrimination in 1947. By 1948, had some of that subsided? Did you still see some evidence that he was being discriminated against throughout the league?

Erskine: I was always proud of baseball that it set the stage and put the components together to allow this first step toward true integration in our country. We'd had this traditional separation, not only in the South, but pretty much across the whole country. It was simply less obvious in the North. But by 1948, when I joined the team, Jackie had been voted rookie of the year. So he had quickly proved himself on the field, both to the players that he played with and against. It didn't take any of those guys long to know that this guy belonged in the big leagues. The Dodger fans quickly embraced Jackie. With opponents in the stands in various places around the league, it took a little bit longer. In Saint Louis, for instance, the crowds were still segregated in those days. They had the black fans sitting in the outfield pavilion and the white fans in the regular stands. And it was almost incidental what the score was sometimes. It was—what did Jackie do? If he booted a ball, the white stands would erupt, or if he struck out or something. But if he made a great play, got a hit, stole a base, the black crowd just went crazy.

The hotels, the transportation, the restaurants took a lot longer to evolve into total acceptance. I remember the Chase Hotel in Saint Louis was the favorite hotel of the players. They always voted on hotels every year, and the Chase was the most favored. It was the last hotel, however, to accept black players. Even then, in the middle fifties, the Chase would allow the black players to stay, but they had to take their meals in their rooms. They couldn't eat in the dining room. They did this for a few more years before that barrier finally came down. That seems strange in the nineties, but the social acceptance of integration has had a much longer evolution than it had on the playing field. So, I think sports, particularly baseball, is absolutely the epitome of affirmative action. Jackie was given the chance then. When he was put on the field and the ball was hit to him, nobody could help him. He had to perform, and he did. When he did, he was very well accepted. That's the way to do it.

RLG: You had some southern boys on the Dodger teams in those years. I remember Preacher Roe,

Dixie Walker, and Pee Wee Reese. Did they have more difficulty accepting Jackie than the ballplayers from the North?

Erskine: I think they did because in the clubhouse and on the field is one thing. But when those players would go to their respective homes in the South, they had to answer, "Are you playing with this guy? He's a teammate? You mean you dress in the same place? You mean you eat in the same place?" et cetera. They had to face all that. Their upbringing was so different and the ingrained feelings were so different that it had to be tougher.

Dixie Walker was one of the most popular players in Brooklyn. You may recall they called him the "People's Cherce." He was a sweet left-handed hitter. He was one of the most outspoken, and I think even signed a petition to block bringing Jackie on the team. Even though he was the most popular player in Brooklyn, Mr. Rickey traded him to Pittsburgh to try to relieve any internal tensions on the team.

The history records the fact that Reese, a southern boy known as the "Little Colonel" from Kentucky, embraced Jackie realistically. He knew this guy was a player and a big-leaguer. Why should he not be able to play?

Now, one incident that took place with Jackie that I've never publicly told before is that Jackie came to Indiana to a function for me here in Anderson to speak at our YMCA at our annual dinner. This was an off-season deal.

RLG: This is while you were still playing?

Erskine: I think it might have been just after our playing days. I met Jackie at the airport and riding up here we always talked very frankly with each other. In fact, I used to disagree with Jackie some because I thought he was too outspoken in some ways. But he says, "Carl, I can't believe it." Now Pee Wee had been his best friend on the field publicly and all that. But in Louisville Jackie had a press conference and one of the writers said to

him, "You know Pee Wee's always been known to be your best friend, your strongest supporter. How do you feel about him owning a bowling alley that's segregated?" That hit Jackie right between the eyes. He said, "Carl, I don't believe that." I said, "Look you've got to realize, Jackie, Pee Wee is probably a very minor owner in that, but they use his name. Louisville is still in the South and things are still changing slowly." But it just hit Jackie hard that this man who had helped him so much and had been so publicly identified with accepting him would have any part of a segregated bowling alley. But that was just the way times were. It wasn't Pee Wee's feeling that he rejected Jackie. Socially, it just hadn't moved that fast yet. When Jackie died in his early fifties, I think he went to his grave feeling that he had only done a partial job. Even though sports began right and left to accept these great black players, and rightfully so, I think he saw the social changes coming too slowly. He was not happy in his life that more hadn't been done.

RLG: You talked about him being a special player. I know he was a superb hitter and a great base stealer. But is there really a particular incident that epitomizes Jackie Robinson to you? What kind of ballplayer was he?

Erskine: First, he was the most exciting player I ever saw. I didn't see Ty Cobb or Rogers Hornsby and some of the players of the past who had to be exciting. But I don't think anybody electrified crowds like Jackie. We used to draw big crowds for exhibition games, spring training games, and pennant race games. We drew these huge crowds mostly because Jackie was the centerpiece. We had a great team, but Jackie and his exciting baserunning just turned crowds on. Either you hated him because he was going to beat you or you loved him because you were a Dodger fan. I'd say Jackie was a complete ballplayer.

Ironically, those who knew Jackie before he was signed into pro baseball and saw him as a college

ABOVE AND BELOW RIGHT: Dale W. McMillen founded the Wildcat Baseball League in Fort Wayne to give all youth between the ages of 7 and 15½ a chance to play baseball. McMillen asked Carl Erskine for advice during the planning stages, and Erskine provided invaluable support for the youth league. He held clinics where he gave pointers and autographs to eager Wildcatters and brought major league greats to Fort Wayne. **BELOW LEFT:** Jackie Robinson, Erskine, Bob Feller, and Ted Williams (left to right) join McMillen (center) on Progress Day in 1962. In recognition of his contributions, McMillen proclaimed Erskine "Godfather of the Wildcat League."

player in football and track said that baseball was not his best sport. Duke Snider lived out on the West Coast and saw Jackie when he was a football player at UCLA. He was an outstanding player. He had a brother who was a great Olympic runner. But Jackie also was an outstanding track star.

The irony is that maybe baseball was not his best sport. But Jackie had qualities that would fool you. He wasn't a real fast runner, in spite of his great baserunning. In a flat-out, fifty-yard dash, probably a lot of guys could beat him. But he had such quick instincts to start and stop, and you couldn't catch Jackie in a rundown. They'd trap him off base, and he'd force the best players in the world to make mistakes. They would think they had him, and about the time they tried to tag him he was gone. He would invariably get out of those rundowns. That was the most exciting thing to see, Jackie trapped, because you knew what would happen.

In the early years, Jackie was so quick he would hit a base hit to right field and he would round first so far that the right fielder would throw behind him to pick him off first. Jackie would always go on to second base. It became funny because we would have all these good arms in right field, and when Jackie would get a base hit, he'd round first so far that they could pick him off easily. But they knew what would happen if they threw behind him, so they would just throw to second and forget it.

RLG: Of course the best arm in right field in those years was Carl Furillo on your own Dodger team.

Erskine: Yes, that's true. Carl also was aided by the distance because right field was only 296 feet, so he couldn't play very deep.

RLG: Jackie Robinson was twenty-eight by the time that he entered the major leagues because of service in World War II. He only had ten seasons in the major leagues. Was he the best player you ever played with?

Erskine: I think he was the best all-around player when you add in not only the skills on the field but also the intensity that he brought to the game. When Jackie's years added up to the point where he couldn't play every day, he would save himself for the bigger games, the games that were the pennant-contending games. When he was not in the lineup, somehow there was a different feeling. But when he was in the lineup, there was an intensity that he brought to the team. It was a competitive, strong, intense feeling about winning and about doing your best. In fact, he used to take exception to our manager, Walt Alston, because Walt was a passive, low-key personality. To argue a call, Jackie would be out on the field. He'd look back, and Walt would still be on the bench. He used to get upset with Alston because Walt didn't get excited like that.

RLG: Jackie retired in 1956 before the Dodgers left Brooklyn, and you retired three years later, after they'd already gone to Los Angeles. Did you see much of Jackie Robinson after that?

Erskine: I was involved with Jackie in some off-field activities. I got into banking when I came back to Anderson. Jackie was one of the founding investors in the Freedom National Bank in Harlem and used to write or call me occasionally about his involvement as a founding director of that bank. It was designed to give low-cost housing loans and a lot of assistance to that area of Harlem.

Jackie once came to Indiana and did something unique with me in Fort Wayne. Dale W. McMillen, who was the owner and founder of Central Soya, started a league in Fort Wayne called Wildcat Baseball. It was for all of the kids that couldn't make Little League. Mr. McMillen was a philanthropist who gave the parks, churches, and schools in Fort Wayne a boost many times. So at McMillen Park, Jackie Robinson and I used to go out and do clinics for all the kids in Fort Wayne in the Wildcat program, and Mr. Mac dubbed us the Godfathers of Wildcat Baseball. I'm talking about five thousand kids.

Then Mr. Mac asked me to get Bob Feller one

year, and then another year it was Ted Williams. One day—and I have a picture of this—in the early sixties at McMillen Park, Bob Feller is pitching to Ted Williams, and Jackie is at second, and I'm in the outfield for five thousand Wildcat kids. Jackie gave himself to youth of all races, and he had an intense feeling about doing the right thing. He used his position as a baseball star to promote patriotism and a good, solid lifestyle. He was a religious person who had been raised by a Christian mother. All those things added up to make Jackie a quality American hero, not just a baseball star.

RLG: Branch Rickey brought both of you to major league baseball and particularly in bringing Jackie Robinson up, he was an innovator or a pioneer. What do you remember most about Mr. Rickey?
Erskine: Mr. Rickey probably was the most influential person, outside of my own family, in my life. You can imagine a kid of nineteen being signed by this major league executive who was a very imposing person with an eloquent vocabulary. He was a farm boy from Ohio and spun this farm background into his conversation. He was a brilliant man and a fair man. One thing he did was to talk to us less

So at McMillen Park, Jackie Robinson and I used to go out and do clinics for all the kids in Fort Wayne in the Wildcat program, and Mr. Mac dubbed us the Godfathers of Wildcat Baseball.

RLG: Jackie Robinson died in 1972. Did you attend the funeral? What kind of tributes were given to him at that time?
Erskine: I did attend the funeral in New York. He was a historic figure, and I always sensed that, more than just a great athlete, a great ballplayer, or a great teammate. He was also a close friend. When you try to put into words what Jackie carried with him to accomplish breaking the color line, it is virtually impossible. Jesse Jackson was the principal speaker that day at the funeral. I know Jesse and appreciate his good work, but I thought he made some strong pronouncements describing Jackie. Jackie was strong-willed. He was disappointed when things didn't really shape up quickly for him, and the tone of Jesse Jackson's message was that Jackie Robinson went to his grave still dissatisfied that he hadn't done enough. I wanted him to hold Jackie up more for the great things he did rather than talk about all the things that didn't get done yet. But if Jackie had been doing the eulogy, he probably would have said about the same thing.

about our baseball skills and more about how we conducted ourselves off the field.

He wanted all of his players to be married. I've always said that one of the main reasons that Jackie Robinson was picked over many great black athletes to be the first black athlete in [major league] baseball was because he was married to a solid, beautiful, intelligent lady named Rachel. She was a steadying force for Jackie. I believe Mr. Rickey saw that in Jackie's total picture. I think that it was one of the strong reasons why he finally picked Jackie.
RLG: You were a small-town boy from Indiana. What was it like trying to adjust to life in the big city?
Erskine: Well, Betty and I had been married in 1947 right after my first full season in the minors. We were just kids going to this foreign country, Brooklyn. First, we had to learn the language. In Brooklyn, the neighborhoods are like small towns. A big city often gets a bad rap that it's cold-blooded and uncaring, but we had great neighbors who still write to us and babysitters who sat with our kids. We still have a lot of close friends in Brooklyn.

Erskine battled a weight problem while playing with the Dodgers—he couldn't keep the pounds on during the summer months. That meant a second breakfast of soup.

It took two or three years to get through that comfort zone there that made us feel good.

It was scary in the beginning. I used to get lost every night going home from the ballpark. I couldn't find my way to my house in Brooklyn, and I wandered around the place. Once I got to know the city and people got to know us, we realized we had settled into a wonderful, almost small-town experience in Brooklyn. I still get a lot of mail from there.

The physician who took care of our kids, Dr. Morris Steiner, died recently, but I've often said that when my oldest son, Danny, who is in his forties, gets a cold my wife still wants to call Dr. Steiner. We had these close ties in Brooklyn just like my hometown of Anderson. It wasn't as tough as it might seem.

What was hard was pitching in Yankee Stadium to seventy thousand people the first time I went there. When I was standing on the mound, I

thought to myself, there's more people here today than live in Anderson, Indiana. I had to get accustomed to some of the grandiose things you'd see in New York and how big the city was and how many people were crammed in there. As far as the personal relationships there, it was very rich.

RLG: You played with another Hoosier on that Brooklyn team—Gil Hodges from southern Indiana. What was Gil Hodges like?

Erskine: Gil was signed by Mr. Rickey, but he was also scouted by the same scout that scouted me. Some people in the Indianapolis area would remember Stanley Feezle. He was a sporting goods dealer and a basketball official, and he scouted part-time for the Dodgers. He scouted me in high school, but before that he had scouted Gil Hodges down in Petersburg and signed Gil a couple of years ahead of me. Gil was one of those ideal kind of ballplayers. I think if I were a manager, I'd want people like Hodges. He didn't say much; he was always playing; he seldom got hurt; he had good power; and he was one guy that when he fell into a slump with the bat, he would still field like crazy. He was an outstanding fielder. With many guys, their fielding suffers when they are in a batting slump. Not Hodges; he was excellent in fielding.

Gil had a lot of these prolonged batting slumps, and when he took a lot of third strikes it drove us crazy. One year he struck out more than one hundred times, and seventy or more times he took the third strike. The marvelous thing about this experience with him was that the fans in Brooklyn would boo anybody. They'd boo you because they loved you or they hated you—you couldn't tell which always. But with his quiet personality and his strong performance defensively, and his presence—he was a big man—they would not boo Hodges, even in his worst slumps. Baseball men would shake their heads because even DiMaggio was booed in Yankee Stadium and Stan Musial in Saint Louis on bad days late in their years, but never Hodges.

RLG: Hodges apparently was very much loved by the Brooklyn fans.

Erskine: Well, there's a couple of reasons for it. One was his wonderful demeanor on the field; he was always breaking up fights. In fact, he helped Jackie a lot by just being there and being respected by the players, and he kept the climate cool on the field. But he also did the ultimate. He married a Brooklyn girl, and he left Indiana and took up residence permanently in Brooklyn. Now they put their arms around him forever for that. But he was a solid player. Many of us agonized that he was not elected into baseball's Hall of Fame in Cooperstown. He and I were the first two players in the Indiana Baseball Hall of Fame when it was first started a few years ago.

Gil and I were always close. Whenever I would warm up to pitch, our organist, Gladys Gooding, would play "Back Home Again in Indiana," and I would glance up at the booth where she was playing. Whenever Hodges would get a hit or a home run, she would play it as well. In Brooklyn, when Gil died, we were walking out as pallbearers, and the organist in that church played "Back Home Again in Indiana," and I just about lost it. At that moment, all of that flooded back to me—those days on the field with Gil, our relationship as good friends, both being from Indiana, both being scouted by the same guy, etc. I was walking out behind the casket with that song being played, and Howard Cosell was outside with his TV crew. He stuck a mike in my face, and it was the only time in my life I had ever refused an interview. I couldn't do it, and I said, "Howard, please excuse me."

RLG: You had a great career in the major leagues. Now that you reflect back on it—what did baseball do for you that has contributed to your life?

Erskine: The Dodger organization was shot through with outstanding players. They had twenty-five farm teams, so they had almost eight hundred players under contract. I think what baseball taught me very early was about competition. Even though it was painful sometimes to see so many good arms, so many good athletes in spring training. How will they ever see me, how will I ever emerge to be noticed because you are just one of so many? I think young people today miss that in life. I think we coddle them too much about competition, and so many things are subsidized. That's why I'm not in favor of class basketball. I want them to play for the real prize and know that the competition is tough. Just like the Olympics, we don't make it easier for the little countries to win a gold medal just because they haven't won one before. You have got to go against the best and when you get it that means the most. I think that's what my life in baseball taught me.

Competition, while it's not an easy thing to face, is what brings out the best. I know that from some of the challenges I had in baseball. I was a small kid from Anderson, Indiana. I didn't see myself as a giant killer or a major league all-star or a Hall of Famer. I was just trying to do my job and hoping I didn't do badly. But in the process I got pushed to do some things I never dreamed that I would be able to do. I set a World Series strikeout record of fourteen against the Yankees, one of the best-hitting teams of all time. That's because I failed in my first start in Yankee Stadium, and I was determined not to fail again. I'd been pushed so hard to do more and do better that I did something I didn't think that I could ever do. I think that's what baseball does. It demonstrates that people don't know how good they are until they are really tested and pushed and until they really have got to grind it out. Then ordinary people do a lot of extraordinary things.

DAN PATCH — THE WORLD'S MOST FAMOUS PACER,
TIME 1:55

An American Sports Icon
Indiana's Dan Patch
Gerald Waite

Sports icons, produced, directed,

and merchandised by the media, are a familiar part of today's American landscape. From Michael Jordan for Nike to Jeff Gordon for Pepsi, prominent sports figures lend their names to products advertised as must-have items to the American public. But how many people know that one of the first successfully merchandised sports figures came from Indiana at a time when Babe Ruth's Louisville Sluggers were still Kentucky forest?

Before television and almost before moving pictures, one of the nation's greatest sports icons of all time endorsed cigars, children's toys, watches, washing machines, gasoline engines, livestock feeds, and a newfangled contraption known as an automobile. Billed as "kindhearted, generous, and a staunch Methodist who never performed on a Sunday," this idol of the American public toured thousands of miles each year in his private railway car. Meeting fans at every stop, he demonstrated his unique physical abilities, in good weather or bad, for the assembled throngs of thousands—but he never gave an interview or signed an autograph. This athlete, known as the "Epitome of Excellence in American Sports," was none other than Indiana's own horse-racing legend, Dan Patch.

Born in Oxford, Indiana, in 1896 to the mare Zelica, owned by local storekeeper Daniel Messner Jr., Dan Patch (named by combining the first name of his owner with a shortened form of the last name of his sire, Joe Patchen) typified the classic American rags-to-riches tale. At birth his legs were so crooked that he required human assistance to stand up and nurse. Some of Messner's neighbors suggested that the horse be put out of its misery. Most of the townspeople called the colt "Messner's Folly." (Ten years later, these same naysayers bragged about their first-hand knowledge of this wonder horse.)

At first even Dan Patch's owner had doubts: one account states that Messner tried to trade the colt for another in the stable of local livery owner John Wattles. When Wattles refused, Messner paid him to train the colt during the summers of 1899 and 1900. It was in all likelihood the patience and foresight of the septuagenarian Wattles that really produced the "Miracle Horse." Even though Dan Patch showed himself to be game and possessed of some speed, Wattles worked the colt slowly and easily until the horse had achieved full growth at age four. At that age Dan Patch stood as an excellent specimen of horseflesh, standing sixteen hands tall (sixty-four inches) at the withers or base of the neck and weighing in at a hefty 1,165 pounds. He participated in his first harness race on August 30, 1900, in Boswell, Indiana, with reports indicating that he outclassed his competition.

In harness racing, the jockey rides not on the horse's back but instead in a sulky pulled by the horse. Horses used in this form of racing are called Standardbreds and are divided into two groups: pacers and trotters. A pacer (as Dan Patch was) moves its legs laterally, right front and right hind, then left front and left hind, striking the ground simultaneously. A trotter moves its legs diagonally, right front and left hind, then left front and right hind, again striking the ground simultaneously. At the turn of the century, racing was done in heats. Riders warmed up their horses for a few fast miles and then ran a series of one-mile contests until one horse had won a clear majority, usually three out of five heats.

In a racing career spanning nearly a decade, Dan Patch lost only two heats and never lost a race. The first of those two losses occurred in 1900 in his second start, at Lafayette, Indiana, against what was termed "real competition." In the first heat, Dan Patch started at the back of the field and was dead last at the beginning of the homestretch. Racing accounts said that he passed horses as if they were standing still but lost by a nose to the favorite, Milo S. No one, not even hometown admirers, had dared bet on him. To everyone's surprise, however, Dan Patch captured the next three heats. The other loss in a heat occurred a year later at Brighton Beach. In that instance judges disciplined Dan Patch's driver for "not driving to win," and the crowd nearly lynched the hapless man.

In 1900, as now, harness racing had a class system in which better horses could be "staked" or paid in advance into higher-caliber races that moved from city to city on what is called the Grand Circuit. Encouraged by his horse's early success, Messner wrote Myron McHenry, a New York horse trainer, and asked that he train Dan Patch and race him at the 1901 Grand Circuit meets. Believing that this was just another small-town horse enthusiast with a fast buggy horse, McHenry tried to discourage Messner by telling him of the expense involved and the great odds against any success. But the Oxford storekeeper persevered. Messner shipped Dan Patch to McHenry, and the pacer made his debut on July 17, 1901, in Detroit. He then raced in Cleveland, Columbus, Buffalo, and Brighton Beach. By August 22 at Readville, Massachusetts, Dan Patch's success was such a foregone conclusion that track owners, fearing staggering financial losses, pulled the horse from the betting. During the season Dan Patch became the most talked-about phenomenon on the American sports scene. He finished the year with twelve straight race wins and $13,800 in earnings. Hometown fans hoped that Dan Patch might race at the Grand Circuit meet at Terre Haute before returning to Oxford for the winter, but no one dared to race against him.

Dan Patch returned to Oxford on November 2, 1901. Twelve days later, the town celebrated its first Dan Patch Day, an event that is still observed. The town band played the "Dan Patch Two Step," written by local resident James W. Steele, as it led its honored pacer in a parade around the town square. Accounts of the time remarked about the almost humanlike sense the horse showed in recognizing friends, dancing to the music, understanding what was said to him, and other characteristics of superior intelligence. No doubt admirers gave him a little too much credit, but the legend grew from there. What is amazing to many horsemen is that Dan Patch could be driven around the square like a pet carriage horse only three weeks after his last Grand Circuit race of the season. Even then, after only sixteen starts, the legend of the unbeaten pacer was becoming bigger than Dan Patch himself.

Hometown heroes have always played an important part in the celebration of small-town America, and Oxford looked to a hero that could put it on the map. Humble origins only help to enhance a hero's image, and Dan Patch certainly had them. As many as six hundred newspaper stories appeared telling the story of Dan Patch's background. Newspaper editors sent the horse flowers, politicians campaigned in early 1902 by handing out Dan Patch cigars and balloons to voters, and all the while the subject of this lavish attention—said to be as gentle as a Newfoundland dog—was running around the town of Oxford hitched to a sleigh.

Oxford residents were shocked in March to learn that Messner had sold his famous pacer to M. E. Sturgis of Buffalo, New York, for the unheard-of sum of $20,000. Sturgis, an elderly bachelor sportsman, had McHenry start Dan Patch in three races in 1902, but by July of that year it was no longer possible to find owners willing to submit to the humiliation of being beaten every time or, if a race could be arranged, track owners willing to allow any betting. Sturgis did the only thing possible at the time, pitting his horse against the clock in exhibition trials. The world's record for the one-mile distance for pacing horses in 1902 stood at one minute, fifty-nine and one quarter seconds, a record set by Star Pointer in 1897. By the end of the 1902 season Dan Patch had matched, but not bettered, the record. By December, however, Dan Patch had created another type of world's record for pacing horses.

Newspaper headlines in December announced that Dan Patch had been sold again, this time for $60,000 to Marion Willis Savage, owner of the International Stock Food Company of Minneapolis, Minnesota.

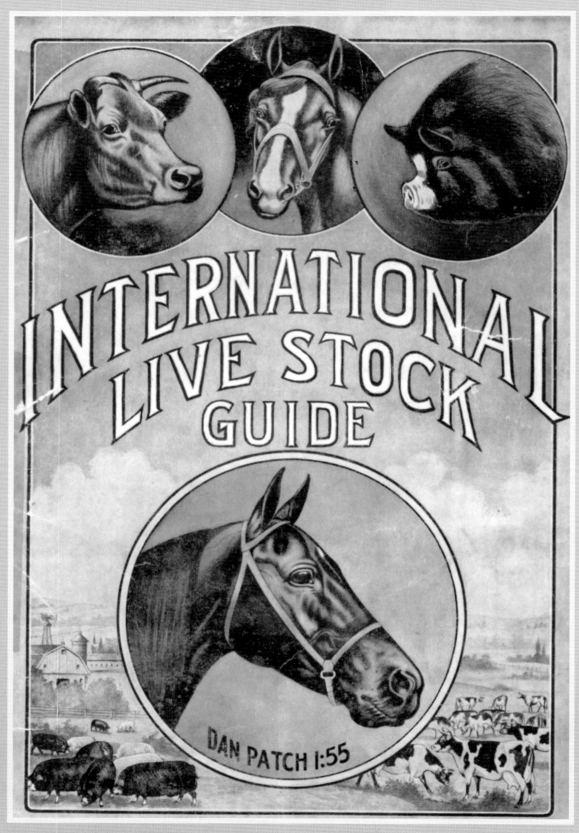

The cover of a 1916 International Stock Food catalog. Even after Dan Patch's death, his name and image remained an integral part of the company's products and literature.

Like today's celebrities, Dan Patch traveled first-class, riding the rails in a private car decorated with his portrait. The car is seen here in front of the International Stock Food Farm's stable, otherwise known as the "Taj Majal."

Savage himself was a rags-to-riches success story, and his background complemented that of his newly acquired prize pacer. Born near Akron, Ohio, in 1859, the son of a country doctor, Savage tried his hand and failed several times in farming and agricultural-related businesses before finally starting the International Stock Food Company in 1886. Beginning in Minneapolis with nothing save enthusiasm and energy, he built the world's largest stock food company of its time and became known as an advertising wizard. It is likely the purchase of Dan Patch was initially just another advertising investment for Savage's burgeoning farm supply empire.

Savage had not bought the world's fastest horse or a world champion of any sort. Dan Patch had only tied Star Pointer's record, and even though there were indications that he might go faster, it was Savage who created the "World's Champion Pacing Horse," subsequently making Dan Patch a household name. It is speculated that the Dan Patch name alone made Savage more than $20,000 in his first month of ownership, with the horse never leaving the barn. As a businessman and horseman Savage was obviously the master of the extreme and extravagant. His palatial stable, which he built to house Dan Patch and other champion horses he purchased, became known as the "Taj Mahal." The five-winged structure had steam heat, running water, a blacksmith shop, and a fire

engine. It housed 130 horses and 60 employees. The workers had rooms for reading, sleeping, and bathing. The complex boasted a top-of-the-line outdoor mile track and an enclosed, steam-heated, half-mile track. Later in Dan Patch's career tourists could visit him on Savage's Minneapolis, Saint Paul, Rochester, and Dubuque Electric Traction Company railroad, which became known as the Dan Patch line.

The year 1903 saw Dan Patch cement his reputation as the "World's Fastest Pacing Horse," breaking every possible record for that style of racing. During the racing season the horse set new records for the half-mile distance, the one-mile distance (breaking Star Pointer's standard), the two-mile distance, and every other type of record Savage could find for his horse to break. Savage's advertising centered on the pacer, and the names Dan Patch and International Stock Food became synonymous. Advertisements for the company claimed that Dan Patch became the "Undisputed World's Champion" only nine months after commencing his International Stock Food diet. The slogan of "three feeds for one cent" became known nationwide in a country that was still largely rural.

Not all was well, however, in the Dan Patch camp. At the end of the 1903 season, Savage's quest for advertising and image, and McHenry's alcoholic brooding, became incompatible. In a move that shocked the harness-racing community, Savage fired McHenry and replaced him with Harry C. Hersey, an unknown exercise boy from the Savage farm. To Savage his decision made sense, not only because the horse liked Hersey, but also because the businessman trusted the young man to drive and care for the horse and, consequently, International Stock Food's image.

The years between 1904 and 1909 proved extremely productive for Savage and his equine hero. Dan Patch continued to better his times; he paced the mile in a record one minute, fifty-five and one quarter seconds in Lexington, Kentucky, in 1905, and then shaved the quarter off in an exhibition at the Minnesota State Fair a year later. Though this new

HAROLD SAVAGE, AGE 8,
DRIVING DAN PATCH 1:55 · · · · M.W. SAVAGE

More than a valuable pacer, Dan Patch was also a beloved pet. Harold Savage, son of M. W. Savage, often hooked the champion to a sleigh and went riding.

Pictures of a young-looking M. W. Savage. Images of Savage are rare and usually make him appear youthful, though he was in his late forties and fifties when he owned Dan Patch.

record did not become official (the sulky used a dirt shield, which was illegal), fans accepted it, and Savage renamed his farm the International 1:55 Stock Food Farm. Meanwhile, advertising blitzes spread out across the country preceding these and other exhibitions. Advance men plastered posters on fences, walls, and billboards, put pictures and stories in every newspaper and farm journal within three hundred miles of an appearance, and even distributed articles supposedly authored by the great horse himself. Stories of the horse's uncanny intelligence, love of band music, and recognition of photographers appeared weeks and even months prior to any appearance. Traveling in his own railroad car, painted white with his own framed portrait on each side of the car, Dan Patch encountered throngs of admirers at every stop.

Savage never required an exhibition fee for Dan Patch's appearances at county and state fairs and Grand Circuit meets; he agreed instead to receive either a percentage of total gate receipts or the receipts in excess of those received on the same day of the previous season. Occasionally fair officials were so staggered by the number of fans who flocked to see Dan Patch that they were reluctant to pay Savage his share. Figures early in the horse's racing career indicate that crowds of 40,000 to 50,000 and more were common. In Muncie, for an appearance that came almost at the end of the horse's career, 20,000 people jammed the fairgrounds to watch an exhibition race between Dan Patch and his stablemate Minor Heir. At that time the total population of Muncie numbered fewer than 23,000 people.

No emotion was ever spared in the creation of the Dan Patch legend. Even when ill and not racing, the horse benefited his owner. In 1904 Dan Patch became seriously ill while in Topeka, Kansas. The *Chicago Tribune* carried the story and said there was little hope, while the *New York Times*'s report seemed guardedly optimistic. The best veterinarians in the Midwest were summoned. Reports had Savage chartering a special train and arriving late that night with International Stock Food patent remedies. Savage and his International Stock Food's Colic Cure were credited for the horse's miraculous recovery.

Dan Patch's fame grew with each year, and so did Savage's advertising gimmicks. The champion endorsed sleds, coaster wagons, the Dan Patch Automobile (which cost $525), tobacco, gasoline

The main stable at the International Stock Food Farm was sprawling, and its nickname "Taj Mahal" was well deserved, as this aerial view proves. Some publicists still felt the need to stretch the truth, though, and produced images of the stable with six wings rather than the actual five.

washing machines, and just about any product associated with International Stock Food. In all thirty products were licensed with Dan Patch's name. Savage also designed and gave away many other advertising specialties such as watercolor portraits, thermometers (an original Dan Patch thermometer for sale at an Indiana antique store in 1998 cost $3,000), and assorted other logo-related freebies. Some estimates say that Savage made about $13 million on the Dan Patch name alone; figures are sketchy, however, and the total profit could be considerably higher. Even more funds poured in from the growth of International Stock Food. The company's business increased from $1 million to $5 million in the first year that Savage owned Dan Patch.

Savage's promotional skills earned him the distinction "the second [P. T.] Barnum." He purchased two dog-and-pony shows from Gentry Brothers of Bloomington, Indiana, and put these shows on the road promoting International Stock Food and Dan Patch. Among other features of these rather ornate circus operations was a movie of Dan Patch pacing his unofficial world-record mile at the Minnesota State Fair. (Flip-card versions of the film were also sold for ten cents. All forty-eight cards in the matchbook-size package had International Stock Food advertising on the reverse.) The shows also featured a canvas wagon pulled by eight dappled gray Percherons, each with a brass plate on its harness that read, "Pals of Dan Patch. International Stock

Food Company, Minneapolis, Minnesota." The horses probably never saw Dan Patch, however, because they wintered in Bloomington every year.

In 1909 lameness forced Dan Patch to retire. He raced in an exhibition at Los Angeles and drew up visibly limping at the end of the mile. He was retired to stud and spent time accompanying his stablemates Minor Heir and George Gano on their exhibition tours. Dan Patch's success as a sire was limited, and he failed to pass along his greatness to any of his offspring. Just as he had marketed Dan Patch, Savage marketed the famous pacer's offspring as though they were the end-all advertising kit for growing businesses everywhere. Even if any of these colts and fillies had shown promise, it is doubtful they could have had the draw their charismatic sire had maintained for so many years.

Savage and Dan Patch benefited during the zenith of harness racing's popularity. America's sporting tastes, however, changed rapidly. Horse transportation and horses as sport were swept aside like outgrown toys in the face of industrialization. Dan Patch's name endorsed the very product that would seal the fate of the horse as a prime mover: the automobile. Dan Patch and his owner did not live to see the new age of mechanization fully blossom, though. The pacer and his owner both fell ill on July 4, 1916. Dan Patch died of an enlarged heart on July 11. Savage was in a Minneapolis hospital for minor surgery when informed of his horse's death. After the initial shock,

he made arrangements to have Dan Patch's body stuffed and mounted for display. Before his order could be fulfilled, however, Savage died, only thirty-two hours after his champion pacer. Savage's wife, Marietta, had the horse's body recalled from the taxidermy shop and secretly buried. During the next two years the racing and breeding stock of the International Stock Food Farm was sold, the farm ceased operations, and Savage's other business interests began a long decline. Today, where the "Taj Mahal" once stood, there is nothing but an empty field.

International Stock Food may be gone, but the name of its icon, Dan Patch, lives on almost a hundred years later, stubbornly refusing to die. The Hoosier Park horse-racing facility in Anderson is located on Dan Patch Circle. The park's annual feature race for pacers is called the Dan Patch Invitational. Writers and horsemen have debated for almost the whole century as to who made whom. Did Dan Patch make Savage, or did the showman advertiser create the "World's Greatest Pacer"? That debate will probably continue. What is known by most horsemen, though, is that Dan Patch was a century ahead of his time. His official pacing record for the one-mile distance stood for thirty-three years before being broken by Billy Direct in 1938. It was another thirty years before the record was substantially lowered, and only in the late 1980s and 1990s have pacers raced at speeds that Dan Patch paced every day.

Gil Hodges

The Hoosier Hero of Brooklyn

Wes D. Gehring

Excelling as both a major-league player for the Brooklyn Dodgers and later as manager of the New York Mets—the "Miracle Mets" who captured the World Series in 1969—his memory is honored today as much for intangibles that never turn up in the record books. As *New York Times* columnist Arthur Daley pointed out, "It so happens that Gilbert Ray Hodges is one of the finest persons ever to wear a big league uniform." Daley, the first sportswriter to win a Pulitzer Prize, later noted upon Hodges's death that the former first baseman served as "the solid anchorman around whom the others revolved. He lent class and dignity and respect to his team and to his profession. As has been written—and rightly so— he had all the attributes of an Eagle Scout. This was quite a man."

job with the Ingle Coal Corporation, conventional wisdom held that the older sibling was the better bet to make the major leagues. Bob was the more aggressive type, while "Bud—well, he'd play all right but he was sort of—well, easygoing." Ironically, Bob's pitching career in the minor leagues was cut short by a sore arm at approximately the same time Gil was making his presence known with the Brooklyn Dodgers.

An even greater irony was that Gil's easygoing nature assisted in his making it in the majors. As a child he was seen as overly complacent about playing various baseball positions based upon the needs or desires of other players. This flexibility and athleticism, however, encouraged the Dodgers to keep Hodges when he struggled with hitting early in his career. Thus, while he eventually became an all-star first baseman,

Hodges always maintained close ties with his Indiana roots, returning often to visit friends and family and to pursue his love of hunting.

These superlatives say nothing of Hodges's Lincolnesque sense of humor. When his classy behavior, home-run power, and grace at first base led baseball historians to compare him to New York Yankee legend Lou Gehrig, Hodges balked at the association with the Hall of Famer. "I appreciate the compliment but Gehrig had one advantage over me," said Hodges. When asked what the advantage was, Hodges simply replied, "He was a better ballplayer."

The self-deprecating Hodges came from humble beginnings in Princeton, Indiana, where he was born on April 4, 1924. Like his frequent World Series rival, Mickey Mantle, he was raised by a father who worked as a miner but yearned to be a ballplayer. Charles Hodges had played semi-professional baseball, and he tutored his two sons, Bob and Bud (as Gil was then called), in hardball basics and urged them to find careers other than mining.

As the boys grew up in Petersburg, where the family had moved when the elder Hodges obtained a better

he initially logged playing time at both third base and catcher. Through the years, Hodges also occasionally doubled as an outfielder. The Hoosier boy who had been only too happy at any position played that versatility into major-league stardom.

Though baseball received a great deal of fatherly emphasis in the Hodges home, young Gil was equally skilled at every sport he tried, from football and basketball to track. That teenage resourcefulness was best demonstrated by the fact that Hodges's track specialties were the 220-yard dash and the shot put— speed and strength, an unusual combination. Moreover, while attending the small Petersburg high school, Hodges played six-man football, a much faster game than the conventional eleven-player variety. Even here, Hodges played the speed position of halfback. Standing more than six feet in height and weighing nearly two hundred pounds, Hodges had, at that time, excellent size for a high-school athlete.

Perhaps Hodges's greatest physical attributes,

however, were his hands. Legendary Dodgers official Branch Rickey, who integrated major-league baseball with the signing of Jackie Robinson, was frequently on record as saying the young "Hodges has the quickest hands I ever saw." Of equal importance was their unusually large size, even for a big man. His close friend and fellow Dodgers teammate Pee Wee Reese entertainingly observed, "Gil's hands are so huge that he could play first [base] without using a glove. He uses one only because it's fashionable." Those monster hands were not, moreover, just famous for scooping up bad throws to first base. They were also helpful when Hodges played the peacemaker. For example, during his first spring-training stint with the Dodgers in 1948, Hodges adeptly rescued Reese from a much larger opponent: "Hodges reached out with a massive paw, grabbed the loose folds of [Fort Worth manager Les] Burger's shirt front and lifted the 200-pounder clear off the ground. 'I don't know where you're going, Les, but it won't be near Pee Wee.'"

Between graduating from high school in 1941 and signing with the Dodgers in 1943, Hodges attended St. Joseph's College in Rensselaer, Indiana. The institution possessed a good athletic program, and Hodges continued his involvement in several sports, hoping for a future as a college coach. His baseball break came in the summer of 1943. While working for Indianapolis's P. R. Mallory Company as a drill-press operator, he played baseball for the company's industrial-league team. His hitting brought him to the attention of Stanley Feezle, a scout for the Dodgers, and after tryouts in both Olean, New York, and New York City, Hodges signed with the Brooklyn ball club, receiving a five-hundred-dollar bonus. Hodges even managed to log one game at Ebbets Field in 1943, playing third base.

Hodges's major-league career was delayed, however, by World War II. Earlier in 1943 he had enlisted in the Marine Corps; he was called to active duty in September. He served as a gunner in an antiaircraft battery and saw action at Iwo Jima and Okinawa. Consistent with Hodges's quiet nature, he seldom spoke about his war experience. But one of his early Dodger teammates, Don Hoak, later remembered, "We kept hearing stories about this big guy from Indiana who killed Japs with his bare hands." Officially, Hodges's courage under fire on Okinawa led to a promotion from corporal to sergeant.

After his discharge from the service, Hodges soon found himself playing for a Dodgers farm team in Newport News, Virginia. The Brooklyn game plan was to convert this former shortstop to catcher. His stay in the Piedmont League was successful, and in 1947 Hodges played in twenty-eight games for the Dodgers as the team's third-string catcher.

Hodges became a full-time player for the Dodgers in 1948 but was moved to first base in order to make room for future Hall of Fame catcher Roy Campanella. Brooklyn manager Leo Durocher noted that when moving Hodges to first base he had told him "to have some fun. Three days later, I looked up and, wow, I was looking at the best first baseman I'd seen since Dolf Camilli." The transplanted Hoosier was now on the verge of his Brooklyn glory years. Starting in 1949, Hodges drove in more than one hundred runs (still one of baseball's premier accomplishments) for seven consecutive seasons. The turning point that season came in a game against future Hall of Fame pitcher Bob Feller. In a conversation Hodges had with his brother, chronicled in Milton J. Shapiro's biography of the first baseman, he dated his confidence as a hitter (particularly with regard to the curveball) from "when I rapped Feller for two, maybe three good hits. And right then I knew—I knew—that I was going to make it."

Many of Hodges's hits came by way of the long ball. In fact, a 1951 Hodges profile in the *Saturday Evening Post* was titled "The Dodgers' Home-Run Kid." Fittingly, the same year as the *Post* piece, he found himself being compared to Babe Ruth as his home-run total rivaled, for a time, the Yankee's 60 home

Hodges (above, right) and Dodger shortstop Pee Wee Reese sign autographs before a game for fans at Ebbets Field. Reese described Hodges as a "man who led by example. In every inning of every game Gil ever played he gave his absolute best."

runs in 1927. Though Hodges cooled off to a mere mortal 40 home runs, it was still heady company for a young slugger. Hodges's career year occurred in 1954 when he smashed 42 home runs, had 130 runs batted in, and hit for a .304 batting average.

Hodges's finest game as a player was also tied to the long ball. On August 31, 1950, against the Milwaukee Braves, he slugged four home runs in a single Ebbets Field game, at that time only the second modern-era National Leaguer to accomplish the feat (fellow Hoosier Chuck Klein was the other). Afterward his playing buddy Reese kidded him, "As far as I can see, all you did was prolong the game."

In addition to such humor, Hodges's performance in this memorable game also brought about a change in his living arrangements. The slugger and his family (wife Joan and two children) had had difficulty finding an apartment to rent, forcing them to stay with Joan's Brooklyn parents. But when this fact surfaced in press coverage of Hodges's four-home-run game, the Dodgers were inundated with amusingly generous lodging offers for little or no rent. Needless to say, the family's housing problems were soon solved.

This affectionate outpouring was an early example of what soon became a long-term love affair between the Brooklyn fans and their power-hitting first baseman. Of course Hodges had immediately scored points both by marrying a Brooklyn girl and making the borough his home in the off-season. The attraction went much beyond that and beyond his baseball skills as well. There was a quiet dignity about this family man, born of a strong religious faith, which was both well known and respected in a borough more celebrated for its eccentricity. Once again a Hodges testimonial also showcases his rich sense of humor. Harold Parrott, traveling secretary for the Dodgers, recalled a flight to St. Louis for a game. Sitting next to Hodges, Parrott noticed that the Catholic slugger had pushed aside his steak dinner. When Parrott asked Hodges why he had left his dinner untouched, the ballplayer noted that it was sup-

posed to be a day of "fast and abstinence" for his faith. "Not for us it isn't," said Parrott. "I checked with the bishop and he said that it was permissible for Catholics to eat meat when traveling if nothing else was available." Hodges responded by asking the height the plane was traveling. When Parrott reported approximately thirty thousand feet, Hodges noted: "Too close to headquarters."

Maybe the best example of this mix of humor, faith, baseball, and fan support occurred when Hodges suffered a lengthy batting slump that touched parts of two seasons. By a warm Sunday in May 1953 the first baseman's parish priest was moved to observe from the pulpit, "It's too hot for a sermon. Keep the Commandments and say a prayer for Gil Hodges." Going beyond prayers, Brooklyn and his Indiana hometown sent him countless letters of encouragement, religious medals, and other good-luck objects. More amazingly the Dodgers' sometimes rabid fans never rode Hodges during this rough period. His teammate and fellow Hoosier Carl Erskine called it "probably the most unusual incident in Brooklyn baseball history. I saw Joe DiMaggio booed in Yankee Stadium and Stan Musial booed in St. Louis. But the Brooklyn fans cheered for Gil."

In a phone interview, Erskine, a native of Anderson, Indiana, reiterated Hodges's special status to both fans and teammates. According to Erskine, the big first baseman constantly provided "stability and insight in just a few words." By the way, all that fan support during his batting slump ultimately paid off. Hodges turned things around in 1953, hitting over .300 for the first time in his career, as well as knocking in 122 runs.

Though Hodges was an adopted Brooklynite, part of his aura of class and dignity was tied to his no-nonsense Indiana background. Indeed, Hodges and Erskine were so associated with the Hoosier State that Ebbets Field organist Gladys Gooding played "(Back Home Again in) Indiana" whenever Hodges homered or Erskine warmed up to pitch. In Erskine's autobiographical *Tales from the Dodger Dugout*, he added, "Gil and I both had

TOP: Hodges started his career with the Dodgers as a catcher. Here he shows his form along with Bruce Edwards and Bobby Bragan. **BOTTOM, LEFT:** Although he hit forty home runs in 1951, Hodges's penchant for the long ball also resulted in his striking out ninety-nine times, which led the league. **BOTTOM, CENTER:** Hodges crosses the plate after one of the 370 home runs he hit during his career. His final round-tripper came as a member of the New York Mets on August 3, 1962. **BOTTOM, RIGHT:** Displaying the murderous tools of their trade are (left to right) sluggers Hodges, Roy Campanella, and Duke Snider.

Of the Brooklyn Dodgers in this photograph, only Hodges, at right, is not in the National Baseball Hall of Fame. The other Dodger greats are (left to right) Snider, Jackie Robinson, Campanella, and Reese.

with several players (including Gehrig). Though now eclipsed, another of Hodges's still-impressive records involved home runs, too. For many years he held the National League mark for most career grand slams (fourteen). On the way to season records for double plays by a first baseman, Hodges won several of baseball's annual Gold Glove Awards for being the best at his position. His career batting average for six All-Star games was an impressive .333.

More important, however, were all those quality intangibles, forever laced with humor. One such incident, during a 1956 exhibition tour of Japan, might have even averted an international incident. During a game in Tokyo, a player for the Dodgers, upset over being called out on strikes, threw his batting helmet on the ground so hard that it bounced to the top of the Brooklyn dugout. The large Japanese crowd became deathly silent. For a culture steeped in politeness and honor, this was a shocking embarrassment—both to the game and the presiding umpire. Hodges, who had entertained Japanese crowds earlier in the tour with some baseball miming, defused the tension with a bit of physical comedy that would have done fellow Hoosier Red Skelton

proud: "Gil popped out from the bench, leaped up on the dugout roof and began to approach the helmet stealthily, as though it were some kind of dangerous viper. He circled it warily, allowing time for the Japanese in the stands to understand what he was doing. Then, after making a few tentative stabs at the helmet, he pounced on it, threw it back on the field, and finished the scene by doing a swan dive off the dugout roof." In response to his antics, the Japanese crowd gave Hodges a ten-minute ovation.

The Dodgers' 1957 move to Los Angeles was as hard on Hodges as it was on Brooklyn. Now in the twilight of his playing career, he found it difficult to leave his transplanted home. While there were a few glory days left (such as batting nearly .400 in the 1959 World Series, in which the Dodgers defeated the Chicago White Sox), his career was quickly winding down. Still, New York City got one final chance to celebrate Hodges as a player. After the 1961 season the expansion New York Mets acquired his services. Playing in the old Polo Grounds, once home to the New York Giants, the 1962 Mets were something of a Big Apple nostalgia team, right down to having the legendary Casey Stengel as their manager. Stengel, who had formerly managed both the Dodgers and the Yankees, envisioned Hodges as a future skipper. "Hodges has the stuff managers are made of," said Stengel. "Number one, he has an even disposition. Number two, he's a good teacher. He's helped a lot of other young men. Three, he never criticizes anybody else. And he has never had a stain of any kind on his career."

Stengel's crystal ball proved correct. While F. Scott Fitzgerald said there are no second acts in American lives, the knowing baseball fan could refute this simply by pointing to Hodges. After retiring as a player in early 1963, he broke in as a manager with the Washington Senators that same year. And, in a happy development for both Hodges and New York, he returned to the Mets as manager in 1968.

The early Mets had been beloved misfits, losing

LEFT TO RIGHT: Hodges prepares for the upcoming year during spring training for the New York Mets in 1962; Hodges takes a congratulatory phone call in the Mets clubhouse following a World Series win against the Baltimore Orioles in 1969; a grave-looking Hodges ponders his team's chances during spring training before the 1969 season; and the winning manager receives hugs of joy from his wife and daughter in the victorious New York Mets clubhouse following the team's World Series triumph.

games in every way imaginable, despite the presence of aging veterans such as Hodges and the incomparable Stengel. There was too much inexperience, too little sense of team. But it did not really matter. New York, stung by the late-1950s defections of both the Dodgers and Giants to California, embraced the Mets with record crowds.

Although the team possessed some talented young players when Hodges took over as manager, the Mets still finished in ninth place. The following year, however, he led the Mets to the most improbable of triumphs—both a National League pennant and a World Series victory over the heavily favored Baltimore Orioles. In what is arguably still the greatest turn-around in major-league history, Hodges more than proved his managerial timber by orchestrating the team now known as the "Miracle Mets."

Another of Fitzgerald's sayings has become a popular axiom in American biography: "Show me a hero and I will write you a tragedy." While that frequently happens (the personal pettiness recently revealed about Yankee legend DiMaggio serves as an example), it certainly does not apply to Hodges. The man led the most honorable of lives, both on and off the diamond. Maybe the greatest tribute to Hodges came from teammate Reese, who summed up the man by saying, "If you had a son, it would be a great thing to have him grow up to be just like Gil Hodges."

The only tragedy associated with Hodges is his premature death by a heart attack, less than three seasons after the miraculous 1969 triumph. Like the seemingly indestructible Gehrig, with whom he was so often compared, he died much too early, only two days before his forty-eighth birthday. But Hodges's legacy was an ongoing influence upon anyone who had ever followed his career. As Mets pitcher Tug McGraw said upon Hodges's death, "As long as I'm a ballplayer, no matter who my manager is, there'll be one man I'll be playing for—Gil Hodges."

For Further Reading

Everett Case Conquers Dixie

Barrier, Smith. *On Tobacco Road: Basketball in North Carolina*. New York: Leisure Press, 1983.

Beezley, William H. *The Wolfpack: Intercollegiate Athletics at North Carolina State University*. Raleigh: North Carolina State University, 1976.

Hoose, Phillip M. *Hoosiers: The Fabulous Basketball Life of Indiana*. New York: Vintage Books, 1986.

Morris, Ron. *ACC Basketball: An Illustrated History*. Chapel Hill, NC: Four Corners Press, 1988.

Williams, Bob. *Hoosier Hysteria: Indiana High School Basketball*. South Bend, IN: Icarus Press, 1982.

The King of Speed

Betts, Charles L. Jr., comp. "Cannon Ball at the Wheel: The Record." *Automobile Quarterly* 13 (first quarter, 1975): 36–37.

Catlin, Russ. "The Inimitable Mister Baker." *Automobile Quarterly* 13 (first quarter, 1975): 38–51.

Hufford, Kenneth. "5,500,000 Famous Miles." *Indianapolis Star Magazine*, May 24, 1953.

A Lure for all Seasons

Gifford, Shirley. "Legendary Lures." *Auburn Evening Star*, December 30, 1999.

Hess, Skip. "An Angling Assembly." *Indianapolis Star*, July 23, 1998.

Smith, Harold E. *Collector's Encyclopedia of Creek Chub Lures and Collectibles: Identification and Values*. Paducah, KY: Collector Books, 2002.

Requiem for a Ballplayer

Berry, Henry, and Harold Berry. *The Boston Red Sox: The Complete Record of Red Sox Baseball*. New York: Macmillan, 1984.

Golenbock, Peter. *Fenway: An Unexpurgated History of the Boston Red Sox*. New York: G. P. Putnam's Sons, 1992.

Honig, Donald. *The Boston Red Sox: An Illustrated History*. New York: Prentice Hall Press, 1990.

Stout, Glenn, and Richard A. Johnson. *Red Sox Century: One Hundred Years of Red Sox Baseball*. Boston: Houghton Mifflin, 2000.

The Club with a Reputation

McQuown, John, ed. *History of the DeKalb County Boxing Club*. Auburn, IN: Printmasters, 1995.

The Shot

Hoose, Phillip M. *Hoosiers: The Fabulous Basketball Life of Indiana*. 2d ed. Indianapolis: Guild Press, 1995.

Marshall, Kerry. *The Ray Crowe Story: A Legend in High School Basketball*. Indianapolis: High School Basketball Cards of America, 1992.

A Major League Friendship

Allen, Maury. *Jackie Robinson: A Life Remembered.* New York and Toronto: Franklin Watts, 1987.

Golenbock, Peter. *Bums: An Oral History of the Brooklyn Dodgers.* New York: Pocket Books, 1986.

Kahn, Roger. *The Boys of Summer.* New York: Harper & Row, 1972.

———. *The Era, 1947–1957: When the Yankees, the Giants, and the Dodgers Ruled the World.* New York: Ticknor & Fields, 1993.

Robinson, Jackie. *I Never Had It Made.* Hopewell, NJ: The Ecco Press, 1995.

Robinson, Rachel. *Jackie Robinson: An Intimate Portrait.* New York: Harry N. Abrams, 1996.

An American Sports Icon

Cross, Mary E. *The Dans…and One Was a Pacer.* Oxford, IN: The Richard B. Cross Co., 1984.

Hille, Herbert R. "Fabulous Hoosier-Born Pacer: Dan Patch." *Outdoor Indiana* 33 (June 1968): 10–11, 29.

Martin, D. R. "The Most Wonderful Horse in the World." *American Heritage* 41 (July/August 1990): 98–105.

Sasse, Fred A. *The Story of the Great Dan Patch.* 2d ed. Blue Earth, MN: The Piper Co., 1969.

Gil Hodges

Amoruso, Marino. *Gil Hodges: The Quiet Man.* Middlebury, VT: Paul S. Eriksson, 1991.

Danzig, Allison, and Joe Reichler. *The History of Baseball: Its Great Players, Teams and Managers.* Englewood Cliffs, NJ: Prentice-Hall, 1959.

Erskine, Carl. *Tales from the Dodger Dugout.* Champaign, IL: Sports Publishing, Inc., 2000.

Gildea, Robert L. "A Major League Friendship: Carl Erskine Remembers Jackie Robinson." *Traces of Indiana and Midwestern History* 9 (winter 1997): 40–48.

Shapiro, Milton J. *The Gil Hodges Story.* New York: Julian Messner, 1960.